Preaching and Worshiping in Advent Christmas and Epiphany

Includes Years A, B, and C

Preaching and Worshiping in Advent Christmas and Epiphany

Includes Years A, B, and C

ABINGDON PRESS
NASHVILLE

PREACHING AND WORSHIPING IN ADVENT, CHRISTMAS, AND EPIPHANY

Copyright © 2005 by Abingdon Press

This book is printed on acid-free paper.

Library of Congress Cataloging-in-Publication Data

Preaching and worshiping in Advent, Christmas, and Epiphany : includes years A, B, and C / editor Cynthia Gadsden.
    p. cm.
  Includes index.
  ISBN 0-687-35223-1 (pbk. : alk. paper)
  1. Advent sermons. 2. Christmas sermons. 3. Epiphany—Sermons. 4. Advent—Prayer-books and devotions—English. 5. Christmas—Prayer-books and devotions—English. 6. Epiphany—Prayer-books and devotions—English. I. Gadsden, Cynthia. II. Title.

  BV4254.5.P74 2005
  251'.61—dc22   2005002122

All scripture quotations unless noted otherwise are taken from the New Revised Standard Version of the Bible, copyright © 1989, by the Division of Christian Education of the National Council of the Churches of Christ in the United States of America. Used by permission. All rights reserved.

Scripture quotations noted KJV are from the King James or Authorized Version of the Bible.

Scripture quotations noted Message are from *THE MESSAGE*. Copyright © Eugene H. Peterson, 1993, 1994, 1995. Used by permission of NavPress Publishing Group.

Scripture quotations noted NIV are from the HOLY BIBLE: NEW INTERNATIONAL VERSION®. Copyright © 1973, 1978, 1984 by the International Bible Society. Used by permission of Zondervan Publishing House. All rights reserved.

Scripture quotations noted NKJV are from the New King James Version. Copyright © 1982 by Thomas Nelson, Inc. Used by permission. All rights reserved.

Scripture quotations noted REB are from Revised English Bible © Oxford University Press and Cambridge University Press 1989.

Scripture quotations noted RSV are from the *Revised Standard Version of the Bible*, copyright 1946, 1952, 1971 by the Division of Christian Education of the National Council of the Churches of Christ in the United States of America. Used by permission. All rights reserved.

05 06 07 08 09 10 11 12 13 14—10 9 8 7 6 5 4 3 2 1

MANUFACTURED IN THE UNITED STATES OF AMERICA

Contents

Year A

First Sunday of Advent
God's House Is a Peaceful House (Isa. 2:1-5) 3
It's Time! (Rom. 13:11-14) 5
A Cosmic Kidnapper? (Matt. 24:36-44) 7
Prayers for Worship 10

Second Sunday of Advent
A Portrait of the Christ (Isa. 11:1-10) 13
The Witness of Welcome (Rom. 15:4-13) 15
Does God Carry a Purse? (Matt. 3:1-12) 16
Prayers for Worship 19

Third Sunday of Advent
Good to the Point of Absurdity (Isa. 35:1-10) 23
The Lord's Coming Again (James 5:7-10) 25
What Do You See? (Matt. 11:2-11) 27
Prayers for Worship 29

Fourth Sunday of Advent
The Patience of God (Isa. 7:10-16) 33
Set Apart (Rom. 1:1-7) 35
I With You Am (Matt. 1:18-25) 37
Prayers for Worship 39

Christmas Eve
No Count (Luke 2:1-14 [15-20]) 43
Prayers for Worship 47

Christmas Day
The Beautiful Feet (John 1:1-14) 49
Prayers for Worship 53

First Sunday After Christmas
    An Old Hymn with a New Meaning (Isa. 63:7-9) . . . 55
    A Community of Christians (Heb. 2:10-18) 56
    Detours (Matt. 2:13-23) 58
    Prayers for Worship 62

Epiphany of the Lord
    Your Light Has Come (Isa. 60:1-6) 67
    Called to Loving Disobedience (Matt. 2:1-12) 68
    Looking for Perfection (Matt. 2:1-12) 69
    Prayers for Worship 71

Year B

First Sunday of Advent
    Let's Talk About Time (Isa. 64:1-9) 75
    Bringing Order to Chaos (1 Cor. 1:3-9) 78
    Will He Find Us Ready? (Mark 13:24-37) 81
    Prayers for Worship 83

Second Sunday of Advent
    Here Is Your God! (Isa. 40:1-11) 89
    It Takes Time! (2 Pet. 3:8-15a) 91
    Encounter at Kmart (Mark 1:1-8) 93
    Prayers for Worship 97

Third Sunday of Advent
    Overcoming Oppressive Theology (Isa. 61:1-4, 8-11) . . . 101
    Paul's Last-Minute Instructions (1 Thess. 5:16-24) . 105
    Something's Coming (John 1:6-8, 19-28) 107
    Prayers for Worship 110

Fourth Sunday of Advent
    The God Who Camps Out (2 Sam. 7:1-11, 16) 115
    The Power of a Final Praise (Rom. 16:25-27) 118
    Here Am I (Luke 1:26-38) 120
    Prayers for Worship 123

Christmas Eve
    A New Community (Isa. 9:2-7) 129
    Keep Unwrapping (Luke 2:1-14 [15-20]) 131
    Prayers for Worship 135

First Sunday After Christmas
    Can God's Future Justify Our Present?
      (Isa. 61:10–62:3) 139
    To Be Inside Where We Belong (Gal. 4:4-7) 141
    Breaking Forth in Wonder (Luke 2:22-40) 143
    Prayers for Worship 146

Epiphany of the Lord
    Come Toward the Light (Isa. 60:1-6) 149
    Share the Secret (Eph. 3:1-12) 151
    Christ's Love Is Like . . . (Matt. 2:1-12) 153
    Prayers for Worship 157

Year C

First Sunday of Advent
    Pre-Christmas Sale Hope (Jer. 33:14-16) 163
    Encouraging One Another (1 Thess. 3:9-13) 165
    Watch, Wait, and Wonder (Luke 21:25-36) 167
    Prayers for Worship 169

Second Sunday of Advent
    The Messenger (Mal. 3:1-4) 175
    What to Give the Baby (Phil. 1:3-11) 178
    And You Call This Good News? (Luke 3:1-6) 181
    Prayers for Worship 183

Third Sunday of Advent
    God Sings (Zeph. 3:14-20) 189
    Rejoice Always! (Phil. 4:4-7) 192
    Concrete Compassion (Luke 3:7-18) 194
    Prayers for Worship 196

Fourth Sunday of Advent
  Who Would Have Ever Thought? (Micah 5:2-5a) . . 201
  The Mystery Ahead (Heb. 10:5-10) 203
  Mary's Song (Luke 1:39-45 [46-55]) 205
  Prayers for Worship 208

Christmas Eve
  The Christmas Eve Zoo (Luke 2:1-14 [15-20]) 215
  Prayers for Worship 218

Christmas Day
  Word Became Flesh (John 1:1-14) 221
  Prayers for Worship 223

First Sunday After Christmas
  Following Samuel's Example (1 Sam. 2:18-20, 26) . 225
  Be-Attitudes for a New Millennium (Col. 3:12-17) . 227
  Not Home Alone (Luke 2:41-52) 229
  Prayers for Worship 232

Epiphany of the Lord
  The Messiah (Matt. 2:1-12) 237
  Prayers for Worship 239

*Revised Common Lectionary Texts for Advent
and Christmas Seasons, Years A, B, and C* 243

*Calendar Dates for First Sundays of Advent,
2005–2014* 245

Scripture Index of Sermon Briefs 247

Year

A

of our enemies,
in holiness and righteousness
him all the . . .

READINGS

Isaiah 2:1-5

Psalm 122

Romans 13:11-14

Matthew 24:36-44

God's House Is a Peaceful House

ISAIAH 2:1-5

A report filed in a newspaper concerning Sharon Stone was most touching. The Hollywood actress gave up her collection of firearms to the Los Angeles County Sheriff's Department, following the shooting and killing of students at Columbine High School in Littleton, Colorado.

In Atlanta, Georgia, a local church sponsored a gun "buy-back" day on the heels of a shooting incident at Heritage High School in nearby Conyers, Georgia. People came from near and far with pistols, sawed-off shotguns, even miniature submachine guns. For every firearm delivered, each man or woman received fifty dollars. The weapon was carefully checked, then placed in an eighteen-gauge brushed steel casket, which was later buried.

Congress began explorations into the subject of violence in the media. The number of violent acts witnessed on a given day of television programming is staggering; it's even worse with 150- to

500-channel satellite television. One wonders about the environment of teenagers like T. J. Solomon. He broke into his stepfather's gun cabinet, withdrew the .22-caliber shotgun, which he fired at will into the Heritage High student body before morning classes, as well as a .357 magnum snub-nosed pistol, which he was relieved of before further injuries could be inflicted.

Our children are not exempt from this. Far too many stories are documented in which children under twelve years of age discover a loaded handgun in a desk or dresser drawer, in the top of a closet, or under a bed, then go outside to "play" with it. Several years ago, the *Free Press* reported that a youngster in Detroit, Michigan, who killed his cousin, was completely unaware a single bullet was in the revolver at the moment he pulled the trigger the fourth or fifth time.

We live in a vicious world—or, at least, it seems that we do. It isn't the world that is vicious; it's that we are, at least potentially. It is said that Adolf Hitler could not hold a conversation. He carried off the veil of omniscience by memorizing huge lists of facts and used these to embarrass his underlings and keep the reins of power tight. This is not particularly engaging; instead, it is smothering. Psychologist James Hillman put it well when he remarked that if we do not learn from that demonic character, we might vote into power someone who wins a TV trivia contest.

> If [a] clue to psychopathy is a trivial mind expressing itself in high-sounding phrases, then an education emphasizing facts rather than thinking, and patriotic, politically or religiously correct "values" rather than critical judgment may produce a nation of achieving high school graduates who are also psychopaths. (*The Soul's Code: In Search of Character and Calling* [New York: Random House, 1996], p. 225)

But God has established a house, not made with hands, where peace is the prime directive. Final arbitration between the nations and Israel will take place therein. The people of their own accord—or so they think—shall come to learn of the ways of God. People will come from near and far to be educated and judged.

And as a result of their willingness to learn, they will be transformed. They will change from a people of the spear and sword to a people of agrarian peace, perhaps taking on the image of Grant Wood's 1930 Midwestern farming couple of *American Gothic* fame. And they will no longer learn war.

(ERIC KILLINGER)

It's Time!

ROMANS 13:11-14

"You know what time it is," commented Paul to his readers in Rome (13:11). Whether they did or not, do we? What Paul meant by these words is not so obvious to us. The dual focus of Advent on the first and final comings of Christ provides a good opportunity to reflect upon time and our relation to it.

This age, to which we are not to be conformed (Romans 12:2), measures life by marking the chronological passage of time: one has lived so many years; the days pass in increments of seven, thirty, three hundred sixty-five, punctuated from time to time by "holidays"; only x more shopping days until Christmas! There may be a sense of a goal in time so marked—getting a driver's license, turning twenty-one, graduating, getting a promotion, retiring. Yet, time seems to devolve into a cycle largely devoid of meaning. Time passes and so do we, and we are gone and our places know us no more. In the desire for our lives to count for something, we work toward making our place bear the mark of our having been here.

When we transpose this perspective on time to the realm of the eschatological, we risk distortion. In the reckoning of the world, this Advent, one in a succession of Advents, should see something that we have done to "bring in the Kingdom." As we see continued evidence of *fallenness* and *unredeemedness*, we can become despondent, as though our lives really make little difference.

This is a flawed perspective. Each Advent is new, and even though we encounter themes of judgment, it is not mere negativity with regard to the way our lives have been. Why is this? Advent partakes of time in the world reflected in the Bible and liturgy. Time in this world is a matter of ripening, of coming to fullness. In his letter to the Galatians, Paul spoke very plainly of this (cf. Gal. 4:4-5; also Philip H. Pfatteicher, *Liturgical Spirituality* [Valley Forge: Trinity Press International, 1997], p. 107). Time calls us, therefore, not to frantic attempts to make meaning, but to expectancy for the revelation of God's meaning. Attempts to make meaning are exercises in idolatry wherein we attempt to create our own salvation. We are called rather to await that which meets us from God's future, seen most fully in Christ.

This sense of time is a freeing judgment, a "no" that brings with it a "yes." It relativizes all of our achievements. On the one hand, it relativizes the good we have accomplished. All our accomplishments, no matter how grand, lack ultimacy and can become idols in our hands. Advent speaks a stern and somber "no" to them. Yet on the other hand, all the wrong that we have committed is also relativized. It is not excused or passed over, but subjected to judgment that holds forth the possibility of new life. A historically oriented sermon on this passage may be preached by focusing upon St. Augustine, who wrestled long and hard with matters of achievements for both good and evil and his relation to God. His conversion was sealed when he read these words from Romans in Alypius's garden. Augustine recounted this narrative of spiritual journey in the first eight chapters of his *Confessions*, with the climax coming in chapter 8. Reflecting on the event, Augustine wrote, "I was mad and dying; but there was sanity in my madness, life in my death" (*The Confessions of St. Augustine*, trans. Rex Warner [New York: Mentor Books, 1963], p. 175). He was met by a possibility not his own, and so by a future he could not make but could only receive as a gift from God. Such is the word of Advent.

(*PHILIP E. THOMPSON*)

A Cosmic Kidnapper?

MATTHEW 24:36-44

Happy New Year! No, we're not too early. We are right on time. Today the church begins its new year. Our focus shifts from one Gospel to another. It is a time for moving on and looking to the future. The future we are called to look toward is the Second Coming of Christ. We are called to look inward, on a personal as well as a cosmic level, to see if we are prepared.

As we begin this new year, the days are getting shorter and darkness comes early. The winter solstice is just a few days away. In fact, the day now contains more darkness than light.

Just as the shorter days cause many animals to settle in for the winter, I want to gather my family around me and settle in for the long night. I yearn for a blazing fire, a cup of tea, and a good book. The cold is shut out. All harm is locked outside our walls. I feel safe and secure and loved.

Maybe that is why I particularly dislike this image of the coming of the Son of Man in Matthew. I want the protector God, the righteous Judge, the Good Shepherd—not God the Thief. Where is my security with a God image like that? The idea that God might break into my life disrupts my safe, comfortable scenario. I am threatened by the thief, violated by the intrusion.

The other two images in this passage from Matthew are equally threatening. The first is a reference by Jesus to the Old Testament story of Noah. How in the world did we ever come to think of this tale as a children's bedtime story? Yes, I know that it ends with a faithful God who is benevolent toward all creation, but it is also a story full of violence and death. God looked upon the earth and judged it. Only Noah found God's favor, was obedient to God's command, and was ready. Everyone else was going about his or her life as usual when the rain and storms came. Matthew's point in referring to this story isn't so much the wickedness of the people as it is their lack of being prepared.

They were unprepared for the judgment, so they were swept away by God. What kind of a bedtime story is that? Am I supposed to rest easily after that?

No. That is exactly Matthew's point. He doesn't want us to rest easily. He is telling us to be awake, to keep watch through the night, to be prepared. And the other image he uses of God's coming is almost as scary as the image of the thief. Two people are working side by side. It is just another normal day, when suddenly one of them is taken away.

This passage caused me great grief as a child. If I came in the door from school and my mother didn't answer my first call, I was horrified that she had been taken and I had been left. To me, these words made God sound like sort of a cosmic kidnapper.

"God isn't a kidnapper!" you say. Hey, I didn't write this Gospel. This is Matthew's recording of Jesus' words. If you are uncomfortable with these images, talk to Jesus about it. This is his shocking call to be ready for his return. He doesn't want any doubt about the seriousness of his coming.

Advent calls us to be watchful and ready and waiting. But for what are we waiting? We are not waiting for Christmas. We are not waiting for the Baby Jesus to be born in a stable in Bethlehem. Christ came in flesh and blood and lived among us because of the great love of God for humanity. But that is not the event for which we wait.

Advent is a time of preparation for something that has not yet happened, something totally new, something that will happen in the fullness of time. It will be a time like no other, and many biblical images used to describe it are not fearful but full of hope.

In that time, the prophet Isaiah tells us, people will lay down their weapons and come to God to decide their conflict. They won't do this out of fear of punishment, but out of trust in God. All the nations will come to Jerusalem where, in the presence of God, weapons of destruction will be turned into tools for planting and pruning. One translation says the weapons will be turned into plows and tools for *trimming* trees.

We may trim our chrismon tree today, but all people have not laid down their weapons. We look around, and the future seems bleak. We live in a world with much darkness. But Christ has brought a light into our world that has made a difference in my life and in your life. What, then, makes us think that God cannot make this great difference in the world? This passage calls us to be awake and prepared. We have the assurance that God is working in human history to the fulfillment of this prophecy. Our task is to do what we can today to bring humanity as close as we possibly can, without having to know all the details of how and when it will happen.

My New Testament professor wrote his doctoral dissertation on apocalyptic literature. After years of work on the dissertation and beyond, he says he is certain of two things. First, we are now closer to the Second Coming of Christ than we ever have been, and second, one of two things will happen to us: either we will die before Christ comes again or Christ will return in our lifetime. Either way, the result is the same. We won't get out alive.

These harsh images of the Gospel lesson remind us that when that new day of God's reign comes, there will be floods and there will be unexpected disappearances. There may be times when God seems like a thief, breaking into our lives and disrupting the comfort we enjoy.

But Isaiah reminds us that when God disrupts our lives in such ways, it will ultimately be for good, not ill. In that inbreaking, God will inaugurate a wonderful new reign of peace and justice. People will beat their swords into plowshares and their spears into pruning hooks, and nations will study war no more.

So what are we called to do in the meantime? Not only are we to live in an awareness of the future, but we are also to live in an awareness of the present. Now is the time to make a commitment to God and live faithfully as a disciple of Jesus Christ. Although nearly two millennia have passed since Paul's writing, the urgency has lessened none. Individually, the frailty of life calls us to be awake now.

We do not have a day to waste in the kingdom. People are hurting and hungry for the reign of Christ in their lives. As we do our part in the kingdom, we need to open our eyes to the people around us, not just circle the wagons and settle in for the night.

In our waiting, in our watching, we have many unanswered questions and tough situations. Oftentimes, we have no clear-cut answers. We are caught up in the tension of the already and the not-yet reign of God. Even Jesus did not know all the answers, for he said even he did not know the day and hour. But he came once, because of the love that casts out fear. He came and he will come again. Even so, come, Lord Jesus!

(*KITTY COOPER HOLTZCLAW*)

Prayers for Worship

CALLS TO WORSHIP

(Psalm 122:1 and Romans 13:11-14, adapted)

Leader: I was glad when they said unto me, "Let us go into the house of the Lord!"

People: **We are standing in God's presence, alert and ready to receive God's word.**

Leader: The night is passing. The day of salvation is near.

People: **We seek to live as people of the light.**

All: **Come, Lord Jesus!**

(*KITTY COOPER HOLTZCLAW*)

(Psalm 122)

Leader: I was glad when they said to me,
             "Let us go to the house of the LORD!"

Our feet are standing within your gates,
　　O Jerusalem.
Jerusalem—built as a city that is bound firmly
　　together.

People:　　**To it the tribes go up**
　　　　　　the tribes of the LORD,
　　　　　as was decreed for Israel,
　　　　　　to give thanks to the name of the LORD.
　　　　　For there the thrones for judgment were set up,
　　　　　　the thrones of the house of David.

Leader:　　Pray for the peace of Jerusalem:
　　　　　　"May they prosper who love you.
　　　　Peace be within your walls,
　　　　　and security within your towers."

People:　　**For the sake of my relatives and friends**
　　　　　I will say, "Peace be within you."
　　　　　For the sake of the house of the LORD our God,
　　　　　I will seek your good.

(*BLAIR G. MEEKS*)

PRAYER OF CONFESSION

Lord of all times, we come into your presence asking your forgiveness. We have failed to live as people of the present. We have wasted our moments, wanting the future now, seeing our dreams as the answer to today's problems. Rather than seeing your blessing in each day, we have looked backward to glory days that seem glorious only in their passing. Open our eyes to our mission at hand. Open our ears to your message to us today, that we might share in bringing the good news of your salvation to the world. In the name of Jesus Christ we pray. Amen.

(*KITTY COOPER HOLTZCLAW*)

ASSURANCE OF PARDON

Christ has paid the price for your sin because he sought your presence in the house of God. When we confess our sin, we no longer have to fear the throne of judgment. In the name of Jesus Christ, you are forgiven!

(KITTY COOPER HOLTZCLAW)

PASTORAL PRAYER

God of peace, you call us to your holy mountain to join the streams of people from all nations who will exchange their swords for plowshares and their spears for pruning hooks. Grant that we may walk in your paths, leaving the shadows of confusion and discord to live in the light of your presence. We pray for all who work toward the day when we will study war no more: for those who negotiate treaties, those who teach conflict resolution, those who show the ways of peace to the children, those who bring your justice and mercy. We thank you for the promise of Jesus' coming again in glory as he once came in lowliness and need. Because we do not know the day of our Lord's coming, wake us up from our sleep that we may live honorably and put on the clothes of light. Because salvation is nearer to us now than when we first believed, keep us awake that we may lay aside all our sorrow and put on the Lord Jesus Christ, in whose name we pray. Amen.

(BLAIR G. MEEKS)

BENEDICTION

You have been privileged to ascend God's holy mountain. Live honorably in the light of God's love. Share the presence of God with those you meet. Peace be with you until the coming day of our Lord. Amen.

(KITTY COOPER HOLTZCLAW)

READINGS

Isaiah 11:1-10

Psalm 72:1-7, 18-19

Romans 15:4-13

Matthew 3:1-12

A Portrait of the Christ

ISAIAH 11:1-10

There are many portraits of Christ. None is better than this word picture painted for us by Isaiah. Written seven centuries before he came, it perfectly describes him.

I. He Will Have a Great Mind (vv. 2-3*a*)

Everyone acknowledges the wisdom of Jesus. Agnostics acknowledge the wisdom of Jesus. Atheists acknowledge the wisdom of Jesus. He showed a comprehensive knowledge of God. He showed a thorough understanding of man. His sermons were deep, his parables practical and pointed.

II. He Will Show a Great Sense of Justice (vv. 3*b*-4)

Injustice was common in Isaiah's time and in Jesus' time. Injustice is still common today. It was the poor especially who were ill-used in those days. There was a need for a just judge, an impartial judge. There will always be such a need. There will always be a need for punishment for the wicked. No thinking person can just dismiss the awful deeds of the merciless as if they were insignificant. Can you imagine a heaven to which everyone is admitted? Can you imagine a heaven that included Attila the Hun, Adolf Hitler, Joseph Stalin, and Saddam Hussein? If "man's inhumanity to man" is never ever punished then justice does not exist in the world; it is only a figment of someone's idealistic imagination. So here, equity for those who have been ill-used is balanced by retribution for those who have mistreated them.

III. He Will Usher in a Great Peace (vv. 6-9)

What a lovely picture here! Natural enemies (wolf and lamb, leopard and kid, calf and lion) live together in peace. It must have been this way in the Garden of Eden! While we will not take this picture literally, we will certainly take it seriously. History notes a period of relative calm in the western world and calls it *Pax Romana:* the peace of Rome. But it was an enforced peace, and not a lasting peace. The *Pax Jesus* (the peace of Jesus) will be real and eternal. We do not see this peace in world situations today, but we will see it someday. Meanwhile we have a foretaste of it in our hearts. In the Bible, it is called "the peace that passes understanding" (Phil. 4:7).

IV. He Will Bring a Great Vision (v. 10)

The first readers of this verse were startled by it. They never thought of the Gentiles as a matter of concern to God. Gentiles were of little concern to them! But here, in the midst of one of their greatest books, is this promise that the Gentiles will come to acknowledge the God of Israel. It was another way of saying that "all nations" should hear about God (Luke 24:47). The Lord Jesus made crystal clear what should have been understood from this text. "Everybody ought to know who Jesus is!" Everyone should have the opportunity to believe in the Christ and to love and serve him. We wonder how the Jews missed that! But then we wonder how we too sometimes miss it. Our circle of concern should be as large as God's! That's more difficult now than it ever was, because we know so much of the news of the world. Difficult or not, our concerns should mirror his!

(ROBERT C. SHANNON)

The Witness of Welcome

ROMANS 15:4-13

You could, with justification, decide not to preach on this lesson. Wedged between lessons that offer much more familiar Advent themes (the shoot from Jesse, the "Peaceful Kingdom," John the Baptizer's call to repent), the Romans lesson lacks the sense of urgency we tend to associate with Advent. What's more, some crucial omissions have been made in the assignment of verses. Verses 1 through 3 are required to add the lesson's necessary context.

I would suggest that, being careful to add the first three verses, this lesson may be fruitfully employed to illumine the Christian life. In so doing, it sheds light on and receives light from the Isaiah and Matthew lessons. As evocative and captivating as the image of the "peaceful kingdom" is, what does it have to do with real life? What keeps it from being simply a dream, the stuff of wishful thinking? Also, as often as we hear of its necessity, what does it mean concretely to "repent" or turn toward the future that is coming from God? This lesson indicates that the life of the community that is indeed turned toward God's future revealed in Christ will reflect the peace that is brought by that future.

Christ did not seek to act for his own benefit (v. 3), but stood in radical solidarity with others, particularly the poor, the outcast, and sinners. His life was turned from self-interest to the future, peaceful reign of God. For us to "welcome one another" (v. 7) is for us to live likewise. We will turn from narrow self-interest, no longer looking for our own gain and benefit, but orienting our lives toward the good of others, and so toward God (1 John 3:11-19). We will be turned toward that promised future. This is to repent. Living in reconciliation and forgiveness, our lives will reflect the reconciliation of Jew and Gentile that God effected in Christ, fulfilling the promises to the chosen people. When the Christian community lives by overcoming divisions, it becomes the tangible sign on earth of God's peaceful kingdom that will be made full in the final restoration of creation.

(PHILIP E. THOMPSON)

Does God Carry a Purse?

MATTHEW 3:1-12

The image of God carrying a purse has haunted me for years—ever since I first read the story of Jan and Susan.[1] In all that time, it has felt as though God was wrestling long and hard with me to ensure that I recognized and that I would not forget the presence being offered. I haven't forgotten. This story of meager but amazing comfort in a hospital waiting room plunged in sorrow has lurked for years in my own unfolding encounter with God. There was even a season when I labored with the question: Does God carry a purse? It is a question I bring to these Advent days.

In that peculiar trough of time between Thanksgiving and Christmas, when predictable and assuring routines fail to hold, Jan's college-aged daughter was in an automobile accident. Any predictability or assurance came apart that day. It was clear that the injuries from the accident would too soon claim her life.

Now all that could be done by anyone was to keep loving and painful vigil. The hospital waiting room was small and packed to the windowsills with friends and family. Together they were rendered silent and apparently helpless. What they knew was a powerlessness to reverse the ebbing away of life.

The loss of a child at any age is devastating. One limps with its wound forever, but there is a particularly sharp and wrenching pain in the death of a child who is finally a young adult in her own right. Some days it seems a miracle, nigh unto impossible, that any child safely navigates the multiple expected and unexpected dangers of childhood and adolescence. Blessed relief, a swell of pride, hopeful prayer, and the releasing of breath long held—each of these and much more fill many a parent as children prepare and make ready to launch into the freedom and responsibility of young adulthood. The death of a child in these years is cruel and crushing. No words resolve it.

The unrelieved silence deepened in the waiting room as unspoken remnants of hope for Jan's daughter's survival grew ever more distant and faded. Suddenly and without explanation, the thick silence was broken. Susan, Jan's best friend, began to rummage and root from one corner of her purse to another. With noisy franticness, she tore through item after item, searching for a stick of gum, a breath mint, a peppermint, lip balm, anything to provide the tiniest increment of comfort. Unable to locate what her shaking fingers sought, Susan resorted to dumping the contents of her purse in full view, on the waiting room floor, in front of her. There, unedited and unprotected, were the gifts she bore. Under the weight of hours of stinging tears, she turned to Jan and implored her, "Whatever it is that you need, please, take it. Take it, now."

Through the pain, we witnessed the image of a friend with a deliberately upturned purse. This is a tender and loving image that has not let me go for numerous seasons. It is a simple, everyday, embarrassingly humble, truly parabolic, and gospel image. It is an image of exposure and vulnerability, not an image of great power. It is an image of generosity born in grief. It is an image of presence in the narrowest of places, in the face of unmentionable crippling pain, where even the act of drawing breath seems too difficult. It is an image of profound faithfulness.

For me, also, it is an image of Immanuel: an image of God with us, an image of God yearning for intimacy, an image of God brokering connection where we feel most isolated and bereft. It is an image of God who comforts when no comfort seems possible. It is an image of God offering what is needed—whatever is needed. It is an image carried in the tenor of a wilderness voice, a frequently unheard voice, an uncomfortable voice from the midst of our anguish and pain. It is the image of a God who does not shy away from the fiery baptism of a hospital waiting room. The Holy One whom we await companions us there, even there, where we expect neither glory nor grace. That is the promise of Immanuel. It is the promise long anticipated from generation to generation and the promise proclaimed in the wilderness of Judea.

John the Baptist cries out for our repentance. Year after year, on this second Sunday of Advent, his message is the same. It does not waver. It will not let us go. "Repent, for the kingdom of heaven has come near." His cry uttered over and over again is to repent, to turn about, to reorient ourselves from our places of privilege, our places of self-assured pedigree, our places of having done it on our own, our places where we rely only and always on ourselves. His cry uttered over and over again is to repent from former limitations in our understanding of the Divine One who is coming, that One whom we await as others have awaited before us. Indeed, we are not the first generation or the last who will be surprised, perhaps even startled, with where and how we will see God. Holy encounter has come and will come again in the stable and in the waiting room. The cry of the Baptist uttered once more resounds among us even today. It need not change. It persists with us. "Repent, for the kingdom of heaven has come near."

We are called to be attentive this day and to repent. Listen well.

Repent, for life made incarnate has all manner of unlikely birth. It will not deny the depths of silence and agony. Repent. Heed the wilderness voices in the harsh places, in the chasms we cannot bind up by ourselves. Repent. Perceive those wilderness voices whose tones will not set forth easy guarantees or triumphant Davidic kings as a shield against tragedies that instantly tear our security apart. Repent. Prepare to receive and to hear the invitation of life incarnate in all circumstances, in every need, radiating with a divine image even unto this day. Repent. Listen in the wilderness, listen to the voice of the Baptist still crying out toward us; listen to the voice of Susan as she empties her purse when there are few, if any, words to speak. Listen and behold the birth, the sometimes fiery birth of life incarnate. Yes, God is with us.

(MARTHA BRUNELL)

Note

1. See *A Book of Christmas: Readings for Reflection During Advent and Christmas* (Nashville: Upper Room Books, 1988), 105.

Prayers for Worship

CALLS TO WORSHIP

(Psalm 72:1-7, 18-19)

Leader: Give the king your justice, O God,
            and your righteousness to a king's son.

**People: May he judge your people with
            righteousness,
            and your poor with justice.
        May the mountains yield prosperity for the
            people,
            and the hills, in righteousness.**

Leader: May he defend the cause of the poor of the
                  people,
             give deliverance to the needy,
             and crush the oppressor.

People: **May he live while the sun endures,
        and as long as the moon, throughout all
           generations.
May he be like rain that falls on the mown grass,
        like showers that water the earth.**

Leader: In his days may righteousness flourish
           and peace abound, until the moon is no more.

People: **Blessed be the LORD, the God of Israel,
        who alone does wondrous things.
Blessed be his glorious name forever;
        may his glory fill the whole earth.
Amen and Amen.**

(<small>BLAIR G. MEEKS</small>)

Leader: We gather in woundedness and in wonder.

All: **We gather both provoked and peaceful.**

Leader: We are here with one another, seeking to be present.

All: **And to know anew the presence of
Immanuel, God with us, story told and story
still becoming.**

(<small>MARTHA BRUNELL</small>)

PRAYER OF CONFESSION

O Wilderness One, in this season of your coming we are
tempted to be comfortable with managing the familiar ways and

places where we expect to meet you. Instead, you come where we often would not go: into the shadows, into the struggle, and into the sorrow that we long to avoid. There you offer comfort that we are reluctant to grasp. Dare we turn around to approach your ancient promise of such coming?

(Martha Brunell)

Assurance of Pardon

God fears not the wounded, divided, or unfinished parts within us, among us, and around us. Quickly or slowly, when we name those parts with open hearts and release them from open hands, God sings with each of us and with all of us together a new song of life.

(Martha Brunell)

Pastoral Prayer

God of promise, your plan for creation is to bring all creatures together in harmony: the wolf and the lamb, the leopard and the kid, the calf and the lion. Give us the trust and joy of a little child, and lead us to live in peace with one another in accordance with Christ Jesus. Grant that we may join with all earth's inhabitants and in one voice glorify God. You sent your messenger John to preach repentance and prepare the way for Christ's coming. Flood our lives with the light of your presence that we may find a new way to live and await with gladness the coming in glory of Jesus our Redeemer. Extend your hand to us, O Lord; bring equity to the poor, mercy to the outcast, endurance to the discouraged, and steadfastness to the weak. Bring to earth the fullness of your knowledge as the waters cover the sea. We give you thanks for your gracious assurance that the root of Jesse shall come. Bring us at last to your glorious dwelling; in the name of Jesus Christ, in whom we hope. Amen.

(Blair G. Meeks)

BENEDICTION

Prophets of old put forth bold and broad dreams of the coming of God. So too may we, here and now, imagine unlikely and precious life—possible once more as the Divine draws near. The opportunity is ours to be faithful and courageous in our commitment to that incarnation.

(MARTHA BRUNELL)

READINGS

Isaiah 35:1-10

Psalm 146:5-10 or Luke 1:47-55

James 5:7-10

Matthew 11:2-11

Good to the Point of Absurdity

ISAIAH 35:1-10

Isaiah 35 is a vision overstated. Could circumstances really turn out so well for the Judean exiles to whom the message was delivered? Surely the prophet exaggerates his case. Yet we come back to these words, as generations before us have, because we sense that God's work is not finished. We hope for still more.

I. Isaiah Exaggerates

Our text comes near the end of the first part of the book called Isaiah. It is part of the transition from the prophecies of doom addressed to Judah in the eighth century to the prophecies of hope addressed to the exiles in the sixth century. The first part of Isaiah ends with a story of deliverance and warning. The Assyrian king laid siege to Jerusalem during the reign of Hezekiah. His effort was unsuccessful, however, and the people of Jerusalem saw the hand of God in their deliverance. Isaiah 36 recounts this, but chapter 39 foreshadows the Babylonian threat that would later succeed where the Assyrians failed. Jerusalem would be destroyed and its inhabitants taken into exile.

The vision of Isaiah 35 is placed to set these events into a larger perspective. It is as if the writer is saying, "You think God did something great when the Assyrians came? Just you wait! You'll see greater things than that!" Readers are prepared for the message of hope to come, even before they hear the warning.

The vision really is a grand one: the desert blooms, the blind see, burning sand becomes pools of water, and the exiles return safely to everlasting joy and prosperity. In a sense the vision came true. The exiles did return eventually. They rebuilt Jerusalem and the temple. Those who returned experienced a second Exodus, again passing through the desert and becoming Israel. But clearly the vision is hyperbole. Things were not as wonderful, as easy, or as permanent as Isaiah 35 suggests.

II. Exaggeration Is Necessary

If Isaiah 35 described the return from exile in accurate detail, we would consider it an interesting artifact, but not the word of God to us. For what it does, it has to be overstated. It points us forward to the further work of God. It says to us, "You think God did something great when the exiles returned? Just you wait! Greater things are ahead."

This vision left the people thirsty for more, for a still better life. Such hopes generated the electric atmosphere in which Jesus ministered. Jesus found people eagerly looking for God to do more. Christians naturally saw Jesus' death and resurrection as the greatest of God's saving acts. And yet they recognized that God is not finished with what Jesus started. We say, "Christ has died. Christ is risen. Christ will come again." We, too, look for more.

We recognize in Jesus' birth a mighty act of God, not entirely unlike the way Judeans looked at deliverance from the Assyrians. Just as the book of Isaiah points to a further work of God, the

Christian looks to God for completion of the work begun by Jesus. Any vision of this work is necessarily overstated because we have no better way to describe it. We lack the capacity and imagination to truly know how God will consummate history. We cannot define eternity in an accurate, technical way. So we take what we know and imagine it good to the point of absurdity. This does not give us knowledge of the counsels and intentions of God, but it does give us hope, hope warranted by what God has already done.

Isaiah 35 is grossly overstated. And thank God it is, for it points us in the right direction.

(DAVID MAULDIN)

The Lord's Coming Again

JAMES 5:7-10

As we have come into a new millennium, there has been a great deal of emphasis upon the end of time, the time toward which all creation is moving and when our Lord will return claiming the faithful, subduing the enemies of God, and heralding the beginning of a whole new relationship with God. Many claim they know the signs and can predict the time. In their claim is the hope it will come soon, for there is a certainty that the one speaking will be among those God claims.

What we have experienced and are experiencing in this emphasis is a kind of impatience with God. We want God to intervene, to break down the things that are counter to what God intended us to be and do, and to claim us for a life that is greater than anything we could imagine or think. We are not alone in this; for the early Christians, this anticipated coming had greater immediacy.

The writer of James advises the early Christians to have patience. He uses that wonderful image of the farmer waiting with patience for the crop, planting in faith that the seed, soil, and weather would all cooperate so that there would be an abundant harvest. There has to be trust in the provisions of God to make the harvest possible.

So it is with the Lord's coming again. There is much to do as we move toward that day. There is much to be done in the world, in us, in the communities of faith. As the Lord patiently and persistently moves toward that day, so should we, in patience, persistently do those things that bring the world and the people of the world into relationship with God through Jesus Christ and that emanate the purposes of God found in creation and in the redeeming work of Christ. This patience being urged implies that we are to be especially attentive to our own relationships with God. "Strengthen your hearts" (v. 8) is the advice of the writer of James. It raises the image of exercise that strengthens our physical heart and body so that it is healthier and ready for the strenuous and trying moments of life. Such exercise enables us to endure longer and with greater sustaining power. So it is that we are to give time to strengthening the inner life so we focus in the right place, drawing on the resources of God which we see more readily, and sensing that entrustment of our lives to God, for whatever comes, whenever it comes.

Patience also implies giving attention to the relationships within the community of faith of which we are a part. I appreciate the candid, straightforward way the writer of James puts it: "Do not grumble against one another, so that you may not be judged" (v. 9). Finding fault with one another is an indication that we have lost sight of the One we anticipate coming. It is focusing on us rather than upon the Lord who is coming. As one friend said, "We need to ask, 'What do my comments about others, my attitudes toward others, and my treatment of others say about my relationship with God through Christ?' " The apostle Paul, in his letters, urges us to seek unity through the Holy Spirit.

The joy is that if we can be patient, allowing God to work toward our Lord's coming in God's own time, we will find ways to strengthen our relationships with God and also work toward a community of faith which reflects the presence of Christ's Spirit among us. It enables us to anticipate a time, whenever God determines it will be, when God will reign and the powers of evil will be subjected to God's reign, forever and ever.

(WILLIAM MILLER)

What Do You See?

MATTHEW 11:2-11

One December, a few years ago, I found myself in New York City for a meeting. On my lunch hour, I decided to do some Christmas shopping. I dashed off, past Saks and Tiffany's, along glittering Fifth Avenue. I was surrounded by crowds, jostled by shoppers. Everyone seemed to be in a hurry. I was part of a frantic mob, intent on our common goal. Nothing could stop us. Soon I was almost running, trying to get somewhere, buy something, do everything I wanted in my bit of free time. Finally I rushed back to my meeting, collapsed into my seat, and thought to myself, "Why? Why did I do that? Why are all those people running around?"

Somehow, that's the mood of this season. There's so much to do—gifts to buy, parties to plan, cards to write. At times, we seem to be running, just like the crowds running down Fifth Avenue. We have our goals, maybe even our lists made. I know that I do: buy a Christmas tree, send cards, plan the open house, write a sermon, and mail presents. We know what needs to be done, so we keep our eyes straight ahead, hurrying toward our goal.

Perhaps we even do that in church. We have our eyes—and our hearts—focused on Christmas. We're ready to sing carols, to move along to the Sunday school program. In a way, we want to rush along and get through the Advent season. It's Christmas that matters to us, so let's get on with it. Let's put up the tree, light the lights. That's our goal, so let's do it!

Our enthusiasm puts us in good company. John the Baptist and his followers would applaud the way we move toward our goal. They, too, had a vision of where they were going, what they were looking for. With courage and dedication, they were preaching the coming of the Messiah. That was what mattered to them, and of that they had no doubts. The Messiah was coming. He would bring change; he would baptize with fire. He would turn the world upside down and bring freedom to the people of Israel. Like us, John had his goals: preparing himself and others for the coming of God's anointed one. He was sure of his task, and he wouldn't let anything get in his way.

Then he met this man called Jesus. And Jesus wasn't what John expected. John expected fire; Jesus talked about love. John hoped for new freedom for his people; Jesus preached that we must all be servants. What was John to think? What was he to do? What became of his list of goals, things of which he was so sure? He just didn't know. And so he sent messengers to ask, "Are you the one?"

The answer that Jesus gave was indirect. He didn't say yes or no. Instead, he pointed in a different direction. "Look around," he said. "What do you see? The blind can see, the crippled walk, lepers are healed, and the deaf hear. The dead are made alive, and the poor hear good news. Is this what you expected? No? Well, then maybe you'd better stop and look again."

John and his followers were only looking in one direction. They were so sure of their goals, their plans, that they rushed straight ahead, never glancing to either side. But Jesus tried to stop them, to shake them up, to get their attention. "Look!" he urged them, "Look at what's happening! God is at work here! That is what matters!" The Baptist and his disciples had preached with sincerity and devotion, but now they needed to have their attention turned from their own ideas to God's ideas. So Jesus answered them: "Look! God is at work. You can see it. Look around you, not just straight ahead."

We need to hear that same message. As we hurry along through this season, we need to stop and look around us. We lit the third candle on the Advent wreath this morning. In some ways, lighting those candles always seems to interrupt our worship service. Everything is moving along nicely, and then suddenly we stop. For a minute or two, we watch the acolyte. Maybe we sing a verse of a hymn to cover that pause, or maybe we just watch. But perhaps just pausing is the best thing we could do. Those minutes are a time when we stop, when God catches our attention and calls us to look around. Like John the Baptist, we have our goals, our plans, our ideas. In the midst of them, God breaks in. As we rush ahead, the Advent wreath gives us a pause, a moment to reconsider, to remember, to see God at work.

As I dashed down Fifth Avenue, I paused. My attention was caught by a sound that seemed out of place. It was the sound of a brass quintet playing carols from the terrace of an office building. All around me, other people stopped: executives with cell phones, ladies in furs, teachers and children on field trips. We all stopped and listened. "O little town of Bethlehem," they played, "How still we see thee lie." Bethlehem, the small, the unimportant. Not loud or fast or exciting. Not what you might expect. But there it was: the birthplace of the King.

Stop and listen today. God may not do what you expect—but God will do wonderful things!

(CATHERINE A. ZIEL)

Prayers for Worship

CALLS TO WORSHIP

(Based on Psalm 146)

Leader: Happy are those whose help is the God of Jacob.

**People: Joyous are those whose hope is in the Lord
their God.**

Leader: The Lord opens the eyes of the blind.

People: **The Lord lifts up those who are bowed down.**

Leader: The Lord will reign forever!

People: **Let all the people praise the Lord!**

(CATHERINE A. ZIEL)

(Song of Mary, Luke 1:46-55)

Leader: My soul magnifies the Lord,
and my spirit rejoices in God my Savior,
for he has looked with favor on the lowliness of
his servant.

People: **Surely, from now on all generations will call
me blessed;
for the Mighty One has done great things for me,
and holy is his name.
His mercy is for those who fear him
from generation to generation.**

Leader: He has shown strength with his arm;
he has scattered the proud in the thoughts
of their hearts.
He has brought down the powerful from their
thrones,
and lifted up the lowly;
he has filled the hungry with good things,
and sent the rich away empty.

People: **He has helped his servant Israel,
in remembrance of his mercy,
according to the promise he made to our ancestors,
to Abraham and to his descendants forever.**

(BLAIR G. MEEKS)

PRAYER OF CONFESSION

Lord, we know that you are the Judge who stands at the door, and we fall before you. We have trusted in our own strength; we have tried to limit you to our horizons. Our stubbornness has kept us from trusting you, and our pride has stopped us from seeing you at work in our lives. Hear us now as we come to you in prayer, and wash us clean of our sin. Amen.

(CATHERINE A. ZIEL)

ASSURANCE OF PARDON

The Lord loves the righteous and watches over the strangers. Those who fall our God lifts up, and to the weak our Lord says, "Be strong!" In the mercy of God, know that your sins are forgiven, your stain is washed away, and you are welcomed into God's loving embrace.

(CATHERINE A. ZIEL)

PASTORAL PRAYER

God of hope, you promised a Savior, and the young girl Mary humbly heard your voice. Is this the one to come or are we to wait for another? He healed the blind, cleansed the lepers, raised the dead, and brought good news to the poor. Is this the one to come or are we to wait for another? The hungry are filled with good things, and the rich sent away empty; the powerful are brought low and the lowly lifted up. Is this the one to come or are we to wait for another? Grant us grace to know the one who comes in your name, bringing your love to a weary world. Give us courage to prepare for your reign of justice and mercy by opening our hearts to all people. May we, with Mary, answer your call, "Here I am, the servant of the Lord." Keep us on your Holy Way; redeem us and guide us to your home where deserts bloom and waters break forth in the wilderness. Fill us with all joy and peace in believing so that we may abound in hope by the power of the Holy Spirit, in the name of Jesus Christ. Amen.

(BLAIR G. MEEKS)

BENEDICTION

(Based on James 5:7-10)

Be patient until the coming of the Lord. Strengthen your hearts, for the coming of the Lord is near. Do not grumble against one another. God has come into our lives. Go forth in joy to await the promised day of Christ's coming again.

(CATHERINE A. ZIEL)

READINGS

Isaiah 7:10-16

Psalm 80:1-7, 17-19

Romans 1:1-7

Matthew 1:18-25

The Patience of God

ISAIAH 7:10-16

I. We Can See God's Patience with Israel

While the coming destruction of the nation of Israel may seem to suggest impatience on the part of God, the opposite is the case. God gives Ahaz a sign even though Ahaz will not ask for a sign. God will not abandon his people. Even in distress, they are to remember that they are the people of God and God will not abandon them. Certainly they had tried God's patience. God had delayed the judgment the nation deserved, but now it must come. Like Israel, we try God's patience. As a nation, we try God's patience. As a church, we try God's patience. As individuals, we try God's patience. No aspect of God's character is more amazing. Stubbornly God keeps working with us and for us— even when we accept God's gifts and grace casually.

II. We Can See God's Patience Through the Years

The prophecy in these verses had both an immediate and a distant fulfillment. If you hold two objects in front of you, you cannot tell how far apart they are. So they could not tell that seven hundred years lay between the first fulfillment and the second. Those who believed the promise must have grown restless, expecting the Messiah to come in their day. But generations had to pass before Jesus came. Galatians 4:4 says that "when the fullness of time had come, God sent forth his Son." Matthew 1:23 says that the Lord Jesus Christ was the ultimate fulfillment of these encouraging words. For seven hundred years they were "standing on the promises."

Christians, too, are standing on the promises. Our Lord will return. Believers have cherished the promise for twenty centuries. We don't know how many more years will pass, but we know that eventually God will do what God promised, and Christ will return. "The Lord is not slow about his promises" (2 Pet. 3:9). God waits so that others may have time and opportunity to repent and come to God.

III. We Can Learn Patience from God

We who would be godly must learn how to be patient. We must be patient with God. God may not answer our prayers immediately, but God will respond. God lets the world go on its way, with all its want and suffering and need. We wonder why God does not say, "Enough!" We wonder why God doesn't bring it all to an end. But we must be patient with God. And we must be patient with one another. All of us are growing spiritually. Some are growing faster than others. Some, like children, grow a while, stop growing, and then start growing again. If Almighty God can be patient with us, surely we can be patient with one another. Hebrews 10:26 says that we need patience. Hebrews 12:1 says we run with patience. James 1:4 says we should let patience have her perfect work. (Patience is a recurring theme in the book of James. See 5:7, 5:8, 5:11.) Second Peter 1:6 says we should add patience to our faith and virtue. Jesus praised the patience of the church at Ephesus. It is a neglected virtue. God is our example. Jesus is our example. Let us all learn patience!

(ROBERT C. SHANNON)

Set Apart

ROMANS 1:1-7

It might be easy to read the beginning of the letter of Paul to the church at Rome and say with some frustration, "How can I preach on this text? It is the salutation to a long theological letter!" It might be easy to skip, but if we look a little closer we may find ourselves amazed at how much Paul packed into the introduction of this letter. It was a custom that ancient Greek letters began with the name of the person who sent the letter and the name of the recipient with a short greeting. In the letter to the Romans, Paul expanded his introduction considerably. He wanted to catch the attention of his readers. Within the introduction, Paul expressed his Christian faith in a short synopsis of what he would later expound upon in the letter.

I. God's Promises

Paul began the letter in the regular manner of letter writing in that day. He gave his name as the sender of the letter. Instead of following immediately with the recipient, though, Paul made a short statement of self-identification. He used the words "apostle," "servant," and a saint "set apart" (v. 1) with the purpose to proclaim God's good news in Jesus Christ. This "gospel of God" (v. 1), this good news, was promised in the scriptures, the sacred writings of the Jews (v. 2). Much can be said on the basis of this theme. Throughout the Old Testament, God promised many things to God's chosen people. Promise and covenant are connected. The content of the covenant is promise. God was and is steadfast in God's promises. There are many examples of covenant promise. In this letter, Paul will write about covenant and promise in reference to Abraham (Gen. 12:1-9). This story and others throughout the Old Testament point to the promise made through covenant and how God was faithful to the promises found in Scripture.

II. God's Promise Fulfilled in Jesus

In verses 3 through 4, Paul gave in a nutshell the truth that the rest of his letter would address: the good news, the truth concerning Jesus Christ. The prophets of the Old Testament had foretold Jesus' coming. The Gospels themselves would later sound the theme that Jesus is the fulfillment of God's promise to God's people. For example, the book of Matthew makes many connections to the fulfillment of God's promise in Jesus as told by the prophets. Matthew 1:22-23 says, "All this took place to fulfill what had been spoken by the Lord through the prophet." (Other references to the promise of Jesus written by the prophets and referenced by Matt. are 2:5-6, 2:17-18, 3:3, 4:14-16, 12:17-21, 13:14-15, 13:34-35, 15:7-9, 21:4-5, 26:31.) In these few verses, Paul expressed much of his belief. Jesus came to earth. He was human, a descendant of David. God's promise for salvation is fulfilled through the death and resurrection of Jesus Christ our Lord.

III. All Are Redeemed in Jesus and Called to Be Saints

Paul, however, does not stop there. Through God's grace, the Gentiles are included in the promise. It was part of the promise long ago. In Abraham, "all families of the earth shall be blessed" (Gen. 12:3). Jesus has come and is the final redemption for all creation. Paul lets the "cat out of the bag" before he ever begins his theological discourse. All are invited to "belong to Jesus Christ" (v. 6), to be set apart as "saints" (v. 7) who belong to God and serve God. Paul invited his Roman readers and us to consider the promise fulfilled in Jesus. How do we belong to Jesus Christ? Are we "set apart" for God's service?

(MARCIA T. THOMPSON)

I With You Am

MATTHEW 1:18-25

We are almost there, we are almost to Bethlehem—and you have been so patient! For three Sundays now you have heard the pain and the hope, the judgment and the deliverance of Advent, those themes we hear in anticipation of the Messiah. This is the final Sunday before we celebrate the miracle of Jesus' birth. And until we do, the color is still Advent purple, with all the humility and suffering and promise it signifies. This is one more purple Sunday on which to watch and wait for the arrival of the Christ Child.

Although he has yet to be born, this morning the Christ Child receives a name: *Emmanuel,* God with us. It is an important name, a fundamental name, a name that summarizes the good news of the gospel.

Way back in Scripture, near the beginning of the Old Testament, tucked in the pages of Exodus, God revealed a name to Moses: the name of God. It became a holy name, holier than any other name for God, a name the Israelites would not utter out loud: *Yahweh.* I am. I will be who I will be. Yahweh—powerful, mysterious, wonderful, and utterly incomprehensible.

Way back in Scripture, near the beginning of the New Testament, tucked inside a dream, God reveals a name to Joseph. It is a promised name, a holy name, that tells of something radically new: *Emmanuel*—God with us, the Spirit of God active in the world as never before.

I Am from the Old Testament. *God with Us* in the New. Now put those two names together. Take Yahweh's name, *I Am,* split it apart, and place Emmanuel's name, *God with Us,* right smack dab in the middle. What do you get? *I with You Am.* That's what God declares in the first chapter of Matthew: "I with You Am."

Now God had been with God's people from the very beginning. God had spoken this promise to Abraham, to Moses, to David, to Isaiah. God's presence with the people of Israel is woven throughout the Old Testament, but never before had God proclaimed it in such an intimate, incarnate way. Matthew's Gospel wants to make it clear that at a particular time, in a particular place, in a particular way, and in the life of a particular person, God intervened in history in order to accomplish the salvation of humankind and all creation. Jesus will save his people, and he will do it by being God with us.

Unlike Luke, who gets ecstatic about angel choirs and heavenly wonder, Matthew is content with the stark reality of a homeless outsider born in Bethlehem at night. It will be a quiet and lonely birth. No family or friends will be there to fret and celebrate.

Unnoticed as it may be, this birth will not go unnoticed by the powers that be. We know enough of the story to be afraid for this child. We know how King Herod will force this family to flee as refugees to Egypt, how Herod will execute his violent paranoia upon the innocents.

You see, the anticipation of Advent—this longing for a savior—cuts both ways. When the psalmist yearns for the One to Come, upon whom God's right hand of favor will fall, and when the prophet Isaiah points to Immanuel, they both do so with their eyes wide open. The psalmists and the prophets are well acquainted with both the awe of God's promise and the terror of its consequences.

Do you think God doesn't know about governments, famines, wars—all the struggles that send this world spinning sickly through space? This child will be born into the world of Tiberius Caesar and our world of power politics. This child will be born into the world of Pontius Pilate and our world of culture clash. This child will be born into the world of Rome and our world of long-armed oppression. This child will be born into the world of High Priest Caiaphas and our world of phony piety and cruel religion. This child will be born into the world of King Herod and our world of dictators who commit genocide in the name of racial purity.

Before Christmas Eve arrives, we need to put Advent back into the manger. This is no cardboard Emmanuel lit with a sixty-watt soft-glow bulb. This is the Emmanuel of righteous justice and magnificent grace, who comes into the world and splits it wide open: "I with You Am."

But why would God come to Joseph in a dream and come to us as a child? What frailty! What vulnerability! What kind of comfort is this for the hungry child in West Africa or East Los Angeles? What kind of security is this for the fearful child in Albania or Alabama? What kind of healing is this for the hurting child in Soweto or Chicago? No matter where they live, children are the first to starve, the first to feel cold, the first to fall from hurt, the first to suffer in the crossfire of terror. This world is no place for a child—especially this child! That's the point, I suppose. Imagine our surprise when we reach out to grasp the hand of God (like the picture of Adam and Creator God on the ceiling of the Sistine Chapel) only to be grasped back with the hand of a child.

You see, the longing and hope and expectation of Advent will be at the manger tomorrow night, present in all the pain and vulnerability that surrounds this child and his family. I pray that you will be there, too. And I pray this, in all confidence and hope in believing, in the holy name of a child. Emmanuel: I with You Am.

(KRISTIN EMERY SALDINE)

Prayers for Worship

CALLS TO WORSHIP

(Based on Psalm 80)

Leader: Give ear, O Shepherd of Israel;

People: Stir up thy might, and come save us!

Leader: O Lord God, how long will you be angry with the prayers of your people?

People: Stir up thy might, and come save us!

Leader: Give us life, O Lord, and we will call on your name;

People: Stir up thy might, and come save us!

All: Restore us, O Lord. Let your face shine, that we might be saved!

(KRISTIN EMERY SALDINE)

(Psalm 80:1-7, 17-19)

Leader: Give ear, O Shepherd of Israel,
  you who lead Joseph like a flock. . . .
Stir up your might, and come to save us!

**People: Restore us, O God;
  let your face shine, that we may be saved.**

Leader: O LORD God of hosts,
  how long will you be angry with your people's
    prayers?
You have fed them with the bread of tears,
  and given them tears to drink in full measure. . . .

**People: Restore us, O God of hosts;
  let your face shine, that we may be saved.**

Leader: But let your hand be upon one at your right hand,
  the one whom you made strong for yourself.
Then we will never turn back from you;
  give us life, and we will call on your name.

People: **Restore us, O LORD God of hosts;**
     let your face shine, that we may be saved.

(*BLAIR G. MEEKS*)

PRAYER OF CONFESSION

Eternal God, generation after generation you prepared a way in our world for the coming of your Son, and by your Spirit you still bring the light of the gospel to darkened lives. We confess that the pain and suffering of the world often outweigh our faith that your grace can heal the world. Open our hearts, Lord, with the hope of the prophets, that we might welcome the coming of Emmanuel. May we rejoice in your salvation and in your holy name. Amen.

(*KRISTIN EMERY SALDINE*)

ASSURANCE OF PARDON

"Comfort, comfort my people," says your God. Speak tenderly to Jerusalem, and cry to her that her iniquity is pardoned. Friends, hear and believe the good news of the gospel. In Jesus Christ we are forgiven.

[The people stand, if able, and sing:]

God rest you merry [Christian friends], let nothing you dismay,
Remember Christ, our Savior, was born on Christmas Day,
To save us all from Satan's power when we were gone astray.
O tidings of comfort and joy, comfort and joy; O tidings of comfort and joy![1]

(*KRISTIN EMERY SALDINE*)

Note

1. "God Rest You Merry," *Pilgrim Hymnal* (Boston: Pilgrim Press, 1958), 122.

Pastoral Prayer

God of light, your church joyfully awaits the coming of its Savior, who enlightens our hearts and dispels the shadows of ignorance and sin. We want to be ready when the long night ends with the dawn's first rays. We want to be ready when the storm clouds break and the rainbow's light shines. We want to be ready when valleys are high, hills are low, and highways are straight. We want to be ready when justice rolls down like the waters of a stream. We want to be ready when the sick are healed and the hungry filled. We want to be ready when all tears are wiped away and our joy is like the morning. We want to be ready when God's glory is revealed, when Jesus our Savior comes. We want to be ready to live so that your reign of justice will touch all earth's people. We want to be ready to celebrate the birth of Jesus, your Son and our Redeemer. We want to be ready to welcome Jesus' coming again in glory. With your Spirit's help, may we walk always in your light, through Jesus' name. Amen.

(Blair G. Meeks)

Benediction

Leader: The King of Glory is coming!

People: We leave this place claimed and redeemed by the One who is and who is to come.

Leader: The Savior of the World is here!

People: We go from this place to bear witness to the light that has come and is coming into the world.

Leader: Come, Lord Jesus, come.

(Kristin Emery Saldine)

READINGS

Isaiah 9:2-7

Psalm 96

Titus 2:11-14

Luke 2:1-14 (15-20)

No Count

LUKE 2:1-14 (15-20)

Did you notice how the Christmas story begins? It's not with the voice of God, not with the song of angels, but with the order of an emperor. Emperor Augustus orders everyone to register at the town of their birth in order to be counted in the census. This means that Joseph and Mary, who live in Nazareth, must travel to Bethlehem. It doesn't matter that the journey is two hundred bumpy miles on the back of a donkey during the rainy season. It doesn't matter that Mary is nine months pregnant. When I was nine months pregnant, I can tell you that the last place I would have wanted to be was on the back of a donkey facing a two-hundred-mile trip through a cold rain! Some days it was difficult enough to get up off the couch and walk into the kitchen.

The Bible doesn't tell us anything about Joseph and Mary's journey. But God has given us imaginations, and I'm sure that you can imagine with me the physical discomfort of Mary during that long journey, her anxiety over the well-being of her unborn child, and Joseph's frustration and anger at being forced to obey the emperor at the cost of endangering his wife and the baby cradled in her womb. We are told that they did arrive in Bethlehem, along with many others—so many others that all the inns were full. Everyone was crowding into Bethlehem for the census.

The census is a growing issue in our own nation. The last time our own government ordered a census, the South Bronx was the most undercounted area in the state. The undercount affected our access to public monies. Millions of dollars have been lost. Plans for education, health care, and social services do not include the uncounted. When plans for the number of classrooms needed for children leave out the thousands of children who are uncounted because they are undocumented or homeless, then classrooms for all children are overcrowded and lacking supplies when those the census says don't exist show up at school. Rooms intended for closets become classrooms. Wanting to be counted is part of our human nature. We want to count for something. When I lived in South Carolina one of the worst things you could say about somebody was that that person was "no count." Not to count means your existence doesn't make any difference.

How ironic it is, then, that when Mary and Joseph go to Bethlehem to be counted there is no place for them and they are forced to go to a stable intended for animals. The fact that they had traveled for two hundred miles and must have been exhausted didn't count for anything. The fact that Mary was in the early stages of labor, for God's sake, didn't count for anything. Mary and Joseph went to be counted, but they were treated as if they didn't count at all.

You know, it's said, "The more things change, the more things stay the same." On this Christmas Eve, there are many people who know just how Mary and Joseph must have felt. I went to a nursing home recently and saw a room full of elderly people being served lunch. Lunch was a cold piece of bread, a cold hot dog, and cold soup. When several people asked to have their lunch heated, especially the soup, they were refused. Another woman, who was tied in her wheelchair, wanted to lie down and take a nap. Again, she was refused. All the people had to sit up in their wheelchairs all day until 8:00 P.M. when they were put to bed. Their individual wishes didn't count. What counted was the efficiency and ease of running the home.

Do all your efforts count for nothing? You work hard on your job—extra hours, extra effort. But instead of thanks, you get more complaints, more headaches, more stress. Doesn't all your hard work count? Maybe you've been a victim of abuse. You've been deeply hurt. But no one seems to take it seriously. It's as if nothing has happened. Their lives go on, but your untreated wounds have not healed. It's as if you and your feelings, your experience, just don't count. Our children go to schools with metal detectors to protect them from violence, but what is being done to protect them from a criminally poor education where four out of five children cannot read or do math at grade level year after year after year? Has the emperor of education decided that certain school districts just don't count?

Two articles appeared side by side in a New York newspaper. One was titled: "Bonanza for Stock Exchange. $900 million will be spent to ensure that NYC remains the financial capital of the world." The neighboring article was titled: "City Hospitals Lose Funds in Pataki Vote." Evidently, New York has nine hundred million dollars for the stock exchange but can't dedicate one hundred thousand dollars for the health care of those who remain outside of the city's financial success. It must be that those folks don't count. Evidently, as far as the emperors of New York City are concerned, the children of God who manage money on Wall Street count more than the children of God who attend Morris High School, or who work long hours in restaurants—washing dishes, scrubbing vegetables, cleaning floors. They count more than those who care for the elderly parents and the young children of the big money managers, more than those who can't find work at all.

Like New York City, the Roman Empire was the financial capital of the world. Rome was a foreign power that had invaded the land of Mary and Joseph. What counted for Emperor Augustus was Roman control, not human rights. So it's not surprising that some of God's children counted more than others. Mary and Joseph weren't even at the bottom. The shepherds were so low down that they didn't even have to show up for the census. The "no-count" shepherds were the Roman Empire's undocumented and were denied any legal rights. All they counted for was counting sheep. Beyond that, they were a big zero.

Although Emperor Augustus has the first word in the Christmas story, he does not have the last word. Someone else was traveling with Mary and Joseph on the road from Nazareth to Bethlehem. How did they ever manage that difficult journey? They managed because, as the angel Gabriel said to Mary in the very beginning, "With God everything is possible" (Luke 1:37). God was with them throughout their journey, hidden in the swell and curves of Mary's womb. God was with them, bound to her flesh with a cord of love.

How do we manage to keep on keeping on on a sometimes rough and painful journey under a foreign power of darkness and sin that has invaded our world and is doing everything possible to make us believe that we are of no account? By the end of the story, we see that those who counted for little or nothing in the eyes of the world—Mary, Joseph, and the no-count shepherds—have counted for everything in the eyes of God. For to them a child was born, to them a Son was given—and given to us, sisters and brothers—and given to us! And the government rests on his shoulders.

We celebrate today because the more things change, the more things stay the same. God is with us, too, when the road is hard and bumpy. God is here, hidden in the curves and turns of our lives, as close as a baby pushing up against a mother's ribs, as close as bread and wine in your mouth, bound to us with a cord of love that nothing can sever.

In the end, the powers of darkness that seek to put us on their list amount to nothing but a big zero. But you and I have our names written in the book of life, inheritors of a wealth beyond Wall Street's wildest dreams—the wealth of love that will not let us go, hope that will not let us down, life that will not let us die. The one who has counted every hair of our heads is on the road with us, no matter what bumps we face in the year ahead. Today, we celebrate because we can count on that.

(*HEIDI NEUMARK*)

Prayers for Worship

CALL TO WORSHIP

Opening Litany

Leader: The Star of David has flowered in our darkness.

People: O come, let us adore him.

Leader: The Rose of Sharon has blossomed in our winter.

People: O come, let us adore him.

Leader: The Lion of Judah has roared in the face of our enemy.

People: O come, let us adore him.

Leader: The Balm of Gilead has come to make the world whole.

People: O come, let us adore him.

Leader: The Bread of Life has come to satisfy the hungry.

People: O come, let us adore him.

Leader: The Good Shepherd has come to seek out the lost.

People: O come, let us adore him.

Leader: The Mother Hen has come to gather her chicks.

People: O come, let us adore him.

Leader: The arms of God have reached up from the straw.

People: **O come, let us adore him.**

Leader: The hands of God have grasped our own.

People: **O come, let us adore him.**

Leader: The Word has become flesh and dwells among us.

People: **O come, let us adore him.**

(Heidi Neumark)

PRAYER OF CONFESSION

Emmanuel, God with Us, you come as once you came and find no room. You come as once you came and your own people know you not. We have shunned your light to walk in darkness. Remove the yoke of our burden. Break the rod of our oppressor, for we cannot free ourselves. Establish and uphold us in justice and righteousness from this time onward and forevermore.

(Heidi Neumark)

ASSURANCE OF PARDON

The people who walked in darkness have seen a great light, and on you this night a great light shines. For to you a child is born, to you a son is given, Wonderful Counselor, the Prince of Peace.

Take heart, people of God! O, sing to the Lord a new song!

(Heidi Neumark)

BENEDICTION

May the everlasting love of God enfold you in blessing,
May the Spirit's light shine before you,
And may the embrace of the Holy Child
Keep you this night and always. Amen.

(Heidi Neumark)

READINGS

Isaiah 52:7-10

Psalm 98

Hebrews 1:1-4 (5-12)

John 1:1-14

The Beautiful Feet

JOHN 1:1-14

You'll have to pardon my indulgence today, because I'm not going to talk about an angelic proclamation of the birth of our Lord, and we won't delve into the theological significance of the shepherds or the wise men who came from the East to see Jesus. Instead, I want to talk not so much about the sublime but about the ordinary; not necessarily about the perfect but about the imperfect; and not so much about the transcendent but about the down-to-earth, the concrete, the messy, the smelly, and the awkward. I want to talk to you about feet—about your feet, my feet, and our feet—feet that have chosen to move and have their being as announcers of good news and as publishers of peace and salvation within the context of a specific time and place.

Babylon was one such specific time and place. The Israelites were captive there, and their history was, unfortunately, not too dissimilar to that of some of our countrymen and women. The

Israelites were enslaved and oppressed in Babylon and were made scapegoats for a government suffused with material lust and impregnated by the devils of classism and racism. Formerly a free people, the Israelites were now slaves, fourth-class citizens relegated to the ghetto part of town. Clamoring desperately for God's liberating presence and power, the Israelites feared that God had abandoned them.

But God had not abandoned them, nor had God turned a deaf ear to their supplication. Instead, the despondent cry of a people for their Messiah thundered through creation and pierced the heart of God. Lo and behold, upon a mountaintop, there appeared the beautiful feet of the bearer of a new message proclaiming a new hope—calling forth a new vision, a new song, announcing a new story where the introduction, the climax, and the end are permeated, supported, and moved on by the knowledge that *our God reigns!*

"How beautiful on the mountains are the feet of those who bring good news" (Isa. 52:7 NIV), the writer exclaims! Suddenly the smelly, ordinary, funny-looking things called *feet* are described as beautiful! The sublime imbues the ordinary, the perfect the imperfect, and the divine becomes concrete and tangible. The feet are beautiful because they are bearers of good news to a wasted people, to a people languishing in despair. God has come to Zion, and salvation is finally at hand.

Centuries later, the image of beautiful feet appears again, this time in the New Testament Scriptures. Romans 10:15 speaks of the beautiful feet of those who follow the new Messenger sent to proclaim the good news of redemption—not just for Zion, but for all humanity. Unlike Isaiah, the Romans passage names the Messenger: Jesus the Christ, Emmanuel, God with Us. The sublime was incarnated in the ordinary and became good news!

Being a messenger is not an easy task, especially when feet are involved. Compared with beautiful eyes or capable hands, feet often go unnoticed and unappreciated. Yet in scripture's upside down, paradoxical perspective, the feet—not the head—are beautiful.

This divine topsy-turvy way of seeing and doing things is good news for people who normally go unnoticed except by those who see them as commodities, for those who are viewed like the old work boots we wear and dispose of when the soles wear out. In God's scheme of things, the feet are beautiful, not because of their high social standing, but because they bear the message of *esperanza:* of light in the midst of darkness, of forgiveness and liberation from the social divisions that constantly vie for our attention and distance us from God. The feet are beautiful because they proclaim that you and I have been liberated from the bondage of sin. We are freed to follow in Christ's footsteps, delivered from the need to hate, enabled to love those who cannot or will not love us, released from the chains of greed, and set free to give even to those who cannot give back.

"Rise up and rejoice!" they proclaim. We are liberated from the bonds of self-centeredness, freed to be with the hurting in our families, neighborhoods, and churches. We need no longer be bound up and paralyzed by despair. The Hope that came to us this Christmas Day has become our salvation. Today Christ bids you and me to see ourselves anew so that we can also see the world, our situations, and others anew. This, my brothers and sisters, is cause for, as we say in our barrios, *fiesta.*

Feet without honor, unknown by name. They are my father's brown feet, daring to preach God's word and speak against inequalities from the pulpit in Small Town, USA.

They are my mother's little feet, proclaiming strength and courage to alcoholics who didn't think they had any other choice or anyone who even cared.

They are the white feet of my Colombian friend and Anglo brother whose way of honoring others speaks wonders about God's mercy and grace.

They are the black feet of my Dominican and Haitian brothers and sisters, who plead for us to live out the kind of incarnational love that is impartial and unconditionally faithful.

They are the feet of our children who challenge us to be color blind as they go off to play with whosoever will give them space.

They are the feet of our *abuelitas* (grandmothers) who take the time to give us a glimpse of God's special care amid the hustle and bustle of our hurried lives.

They are the feet of our teenagers who stand up against the pressure for conformity to the dictates of this generation's "in group"—feet that don't win accolades or medals, but feet that love the Lord and love those for whom Jesus came this Christmas Day.

They are the feet of former drug addicts and pimps who respond to God's gift of love through Jesus Christ by daring to make a difference in our inner cities and barrios.

They are feet that stick out in their classrooms because they teach with love and conviction.

They are the hands that spin the wheels of a wheelchair, generating boldness and vigor for God's precious gift of life.

They are feet that dance with the lonely, lead the wavering, and dare to stand firm against injustice.

Are they just *feet?* No! They are beautiful feet, embracing the spirit of Christmas and living out the good news—whatever the context might be. The ordinary has become sublime.

If we underestimate the challenge and the cost to those who call themselves sons and daughters of God—that is, *familia*—then we cannot comprehend the depth of God's gift of love through Jesus Christ. Oppressed peoples know all too well that there is no *fiesta* without struggle. Isaiah's Jerusalem would not be rebuilt without trouble. The bloodshed of innocent babies, and the suffering of their loved ones, would accompany the birth of the Christ Child.

And then there are Jesus' feet. John 1:11 reminds us that Jesus' beautiful feet were spat upon, stepped on, crushed, and finally nailed to a tree by the very ones Jesus came to save. These are the feet we have chosen to follow, and as Jesus reminds us, the servant is not greater than the master. Proclaiming Jesus as Lord means that our feet, too, might be stepped on, spat upon, or even crushed by those who reject God's gift of love. Certainly they will suffer the pain of indifference and be pierced by rejection.

Yet as surely as we know pain, Scripture says we shall also

know joy. As Mary anointed Jesus, so God will send someone to soothe our aching and swollen feet with sweet perfume and to dry them with her hair. The beautiful feet of Jesus not only experienced the torture of execution, they also experienced the power of resurrection. The Christmas story is a call to a journey of proclamation, an invitation to join God's messengers of good tidings to a hurting and hurtful world. It is a journey worth taking, a path worth following.

May God bless your skinny, flat, big, small, brown, white, red, or black feet. May they be called beautiful.

(ZAIDA MALDONADO PÉREZ)

Prayers for Worship

CALL TO WORSHIP

One: How beautiful upon the mountains are the feet of the messenger,

Many: Who announces peace, who brings good news, who announces salvation, who says, "Your God reigns!"

One: Rejoice, for the light that enlightens everyone has come to the world;

All: We have seen his glory—the glory of a parent's only son—full of grace and truth. Alleluia!

(ZAIDA MALDONADO PÉREZ)

PRAYER OF CONFESSION

Precious God, we rejoice in the knowledge that you loved us so much that you gifted us with your only begotten Son, Jesus, whose birth, life, and deeds we gather to celebrate. Through him you remind us that no matter what happens in our lives, you will be there to strengthen us and to help move us to where we can exclaim, "Our God reigns!"

We give you praise and thanks, for you have chosen to lead us and have shown us the way to you through your Son, Jesus. This good news gives us great cause for joy and celebration. But you also remind us that we are called to follow Jesus' example and become God's messengers of love and salvation to a hurting and alienated world. Like the feet of the Messenger, our feet, too, are deemed beautiful when we follow in his footsteps.

We do not always choose Jesus' path, sometimes succumbing to the way of indifference and self-concern. When we do this, we miss out on the blessings that come only from following the Giver of Life and from leading others to that wholeness. Help our feet to be beautiful in your sight.

We ask for a fresh outpouring of your Spirit so that our feet may find the desire and courage they need to lose themselves in the dance of the good news that our God reigns.

(ZAIDA MALDONADO PÉREZ)

BENEDICTION

Let us go out into the world, empowered by God to be the beautiful feet that live out the good news of God's reign!

(ZAIDA MALDONADO PÉREZ)

READINGS

Isaiah 63:7-9

Psalm 148

Hebrews 2:10-18

Matthew 2:13-23

An Old Hymn with a New Meaning

ISAIAH 63:7-9

This is a hymn of gratitude for the kindness and mercy Yahweh has shown Israel. If we were to compare it to the structure of one of our modern hymns, several verses could be pointed out.

The first one is an affirmation that *God has been Israel's Savior* (v. 8). Whether we think of Israel's deliverance from the captivity to the Babylonians, here in the immediate context, or the rescue from Egypt, or any number of other acts of mercy, the theme of "Yahweh as Savior" is a chord played throughout Israel's history.

These questions come to mind. Can we think now of God as the savior of the nations? Do God's acts of saving mercy extend to nations we do not normally consider Christian?

The second verse of our hymn is the clear message that *God participates in the suffering of God's people* (v. 9). I remember once hearing a comment on this verse that went something like this: "In Israel's adversity, God was no adversary."

One might want to read again, at least, portions of the book of Job, to catch something of the dynamic of the adversarial role of God in people's lives. Of course, the drama ends with the startling truth: "In adversity, God is no adversary."

The third verse has the wonderful image of a *parent lifting a child from danger or unpleasant circumstances with strong arms and carrying that child to safety* (v. 9). A church I once attended was celebrating its one hundredth anniversary. Much of the history was presented on video. The story included comments about many persons in the past who had served faithfully but also included words about persons presently in attendance at the church. We were told that four children come to the church every Sunday but without their parents.

The visiting speaker for the day said to me after the service, "On my way home I'm going to stop by and visit the parents of those children." His intent was not to make a scene or preach at the parents for not attending church with their children, but simply to be an encourager. This unselfish act was made more moving because he didn't even know those children's parents. The speaker illustrated that he was committed to the children of our world and serves for us as a reminder of our call to care for the children.

Visualize, if you will, an image of children being carried from unpleasant circumstances with strong arms to safety. Perhaps there is no greater challenge the church could receive today than to become known as the strong arms that carry children to safety.

(JIM CLARDY)

A Community of Christians

HEBREWS 2:10-18

Suffering has had a varied role in the history of the church. The church has tried to grasp how suffering is to fit into our lives through studying the initial example of Jesus. It is clear that Jesus chose to suffer and die as an expression of his obedience to God. It is also clear that when Christians are confronted with the choice of turning aside from the gospel or enduring suffering, they are to choose in favor of the gospel and in so doing, embrace suffering. What is not clear is the way Christians who are not caught in threatening situations are to relate to suffering.

Some, especially in the earliest days of the faith, became so fixated on a martyr theology that they sought out suffering and death as a guarantee of their salvation and of their special place with God. Marks of identification with Christ's suffering, the stigmata, were highly prized.

Some in our less threatened times have turned away from suffering as a mark of spiritual blessing and have proclaimed a "gospel" of blessing. The triumph of Jesus over the forces of sin, death, and suffering is viewed as complete and God wishes nothing for Christians but health, happiness, and material prosperity. Hebrews 2:10-18 calls the church back to the meaning of suffering without romanticizing the experience.

The primary "actor" in this passage is God. God is the Creator, the One "for whom and through whom all things exist." God is also the One whose loving purpose is to draw many into "glory," into relationship with God. God also is the power behind the completion of Jesus through suffering. It is not appropriate for us to imagine a heavenly council in which a plan is put forward to run Jesus through some maze of suffering as if God were a mad scientist, experimenting on a rat. The writer of Hebrews did not hesitate to place the words that the Hebrew Scripture attributes to God in the mouth of Jesus. The unique role and identity of Jesus, fully human and fully divine, is maintained throughout Hebrews.

Suffering created the Christian community. We are who we are through the sacrifice of Jesus. Jesus did not create a company of disciples who would propagate his ideas; he created a community of people who have been transformed through his death. Jesus' completion (being made perfect) through suffering is a call for others who must be sanctified to share in suffering as well. The humble, oppressed, and despised of the community of Christians are called Jesus' brothers and sisters because they share with him these experiences.

Jesus' victory over sin and death is not something added to the experience of the cross by God. God did not look on as Jesus was faithful unto death and then, as a consequence of his faithfulness, grant the conquest over evil. It was in the very act of Jesus' obedience that sin and death were defeated. Neither Hebrews nor any other Christian scripture solves the mystery of salvation. God is intimately involved in human salvation, not as a spectator but as a participant.

Hebrews helps the Christian seeking to understand salvation to gaze at the mystery from a different perspective. All the theories of the "how" of salvation should be taken together without seeking to fold one into another. The one offered here, that of the "sacrifice of atonement," is sometimes taken in isolation from others. When this happens, the great truth of the mystery of salvation is distorted. Ultimately, the question of salvation's "how" is overwhelmed by salvation's "who." Too much time and energy has gone into worrying through theories, which in the final analysis, are best left in the heart of God.

What Hebrews does is to connect the suffering of Jesus with the experiences of the Christians to whom the message is intended. Their (and our) sufferings are gathered into the greater purpose of God in such a manner as to identify them with Jesus' successful endurance and triumph. The completeness of Jesus' humanity enabled him to be both the example and enabler of the Christian's victory.

(LEE GALLMAN)

Detours

MATTHEW 2:13-23

Do you ever plan your travel schedule so that you only have the exact number of minutes it takes to get from one place to the next? I have to admit, I tend to make a habit of it. And yes, things don't always go as I plan. Recently, I was to meet the youth from my church for a late summer trip to Carowinds, an amusement park not far from our town. We were to meet at the church at 8:00 on a Tuesday morning, and I left my apartment at 7:52, having exactly the eight minutes it takes to get from home to church if I take the route I have timed to be the fastest. But on that day something I hadn't counted on threw my timing out the window. I turned onto the third street before the church, and I saw it—that unmistakable orange and black sign looming in my path: DETOUR. By the time I finally got to the church, the parking lot was crawling with anxious teenagers who surrounded me, not so subtly tapping on their watches as I got out of my car. We did finally make it to the amusement park and the day was even a good one, no thanks to my early-morning detour.

Detours. They're one of the less convenient parts of life. Still, when you think about it, life really is full of them, and I don't just mean signs on the road. The past few weeks in particular may have seemed like one big detour for many. The Christmas season can do that to you. Maybe you take a detour on the way home from work one day to pick up a present for your daughter, or maybe you detour from your regular Saturday schedule to *really* clean the house because the family is coming to your place this year. We detour to put up the tree, detour to make a few cookies, detour to fit in a few extra church services. And just because Christmas has now passed doesn't mean it's over yet. Now we have to detour around our ordinary schedules in order to take down the tree, pack up the ornaments, and put the crèches away. The Christmas season is full of detours, yet it seems appropriate in some way—a little like we're continuing a tradition that started years ago with the first Christmas.

Mary and Joseph certainly were no strangers to detours. It's a safe guess that the circumstances surrounding Mary's pregnancy were not along the lines she had planned for her life. And we all know what happened when Mary and Joseph approached the inn in Bethlehem for a place to stay. There was that big, black and orange sign: Detour—straight to the stable. Then there were the wise men who came to worship the child. As they were preparing to leave, they were warned in a dream about Herod, the king who had inquired rather suspiciously about this child. So they detoured away from Herod and went home by another way, which brings us to our story today. Word comes to Joseph in a dream that he needs to take his family and flee to Egypt to escape Herod who is seeking this child and who will stop at nothing less than destroying him. So Joseph and Mary and the child pack up and head to Egypt.

Yes, detours seem to characterize this season. Some of the detours we make in observing it, however, aren't such prudent ones. There's another detour that's typically a part of our tradition this time of year. It's a detour we make around verses sixteen through eighteen in our Gospel reading:

> When Herod saw that he had been tricked by the wise men, he was infuriated, and he sent and killed all the children in and around Bethlehem who were two years old or under, according to the time that he had learned from the wise men. Then was fulfilled what had been spoken through the prophet Jeremiah: "A voice was heard in Ra'mah, wailing and loud lamentation, Rachel weeping for her children; she refused to be consoled, because they are no more." (Matt. 2:16-18)

These verses are not ones we usually hear around Christmastime. As familiar as the shepherds and three kings are to our celebrations at Christmas, so are these verses absent. These verses just don't fit our story, our images of how this nativity scene is supposed to end. This account of murdered children is antithetical to what we picture in thinking of Jesus coming into the world. After all, the story does not need the explicit description of what Herod had done. If these three verses were removed, the story would still have continuity. Mary and Joseph and Jesus would move to Egypt, Herod would die, they would move back and eventually settle in Nazareth.

But the author of Matthew chose to put this story here. And so as we examine our own detour away from this story, we should ask ourselves why it's here in the first place. It may be simply that it is here because it is true. In accounts outside of the Bible, Herod is documented as a wicked and cruel man, capable of orchestrating such an event. Or it may be that Matthew wants to highlight a connection between Jesus and Moses, whose story also includes the escape from the killing of children. There are several valid explanations, but ultimately we don't know exactly why Matthew puts this story here.

In our examination of it, however, ironically we begin to see what we miss when we detour around it. By putting this story here, Matthew is telling us something about the world into which Jesus was born, about the hostility Jesus encountered, and about pain that just doesn't seem to fit. He is telling us about pain inflicted upon innocent children whose mother, Rachel, would not be consoled, pain so deep it is difficult for us to comprehend it; yet pain, in other ways, that we understand all too well—even at Christmas—especially at Christmas.

Though as Christians we try to react against the idealistic commercialization bombarding us at every turn, Christmas remains a time when we imagine that all might be well, that families will come together and expectations will be fulfilled. And so often this week after Christmas is spent, by many of us, in the realization that in some way it didn't all seem to fit. The news carried no fewer reports of suffering and death, and our lives as Christians, even in this season surrounding our Savior, haven't fallen into place yet.

Was there something that didn't fit for you this year? It may have been something simple. Maybe you searched high and low for the perfect gift only to hear, "Mom, I wanted the *blue* toy." Maybe your bank account wasn't fit for any extravagance. Maybe this was your first Christmas without a certain loved one, or your last Christmas with that loved one. Or maybe your family fought all day, or the forgiveness you'd hoped would come didn't. And part of what makes all these things so painful is that we all know it's not the way it's supposed to be. Christmas is about a baby born in a stable, and angels and shepherds and wise men, peace on earth and goodwill toward all people.

But Christmas, according to Matthew, is also about the real world into which this baby was born: a world of heartache and suffering and killing. And when we detour around this story, we miss the fullness of how much this birth meant. This birth didn't happen at a time when everything was going right or when people were feeling especially good about themselves or when no one went hungry. This birth *broke in* in the midst of tragedy.

Edmund Steimle, a Lutheran pastor, called Jesus' birth in Bethlehem that first Christmas the "eye of the storm."[1] For a moment there was a peace that passes understanding, a breaking-in of the kingdom, a breaking-in that didn't deny the pain or hurt of the world but that happened in spite of it. And we encounter the power that brought peace not apart from this world, but in its midst. This birth was a *detour* aimed straight at Truth—the Truth of God's love and presence in the midst of this broken world.

Embracing the message of Christmas doesn't demand denial of pain, global or personal, and it doesn't mean that everything will fit together. No, the truth of Christmas is this: even, and *especially*, for such a time as this, God is with us. Emmanuel.

(DORISANNE COOPER)

Note

1. See Edmund A. Steimle, "The Eye of the Storm," in Thomas G. Long and Cornelius Plantinga, Jr., eds., *A Chorus of Witnesses* (Grand Rapids: Eerdmans, 1994), 237-42.

Prayers for Worship

CALLS TO WORSHIP

Leader: We are gathered here this morning, tired from the last few weeks.

People: We are here this morning wondering how Christmas has again passed without peace in our lives.

Leader: We are here to renew and draw strength.

People: **We are here because there is no place more fitting that we could be.**

(Dorisanne Cooper)

(Psalm 148:1-6, 7-13)

Leader: Praise the Lord from the heavens;
  praise him in the heights!
Praise him, all his angels;
  praise him, all his host!
Praise him, sun and moon;
  praise him, all you shining stars!
Praise him, you highest heavens,
  and you waters above the heavens!
Let them praise the name of the Lord,
  for he commanded and they were created.

People: **Praise the Lord from the earth,**
  you sea monsters and all deeps,
fire and hail, snow and frost,
  stormy wind fulfilling his command!
Mountains and all hills,
  fruit trees and all cedars!
Wild animals and all cattle,
  creeping things and flying birds!

Leader: Kings of the earth and all peoples,
  princes and all rulers of the earth!
Young men and women alike,
  old and young together!

People: **Let them praise the name of the Lord,**
  for his name alone is exalted;
  his glory is above earth and heaven.

(Blair G. Meeks)

PRAYER OF CONFESSION

O God, in this season it is so tempting to want to pretend all is well, to convince ourselves that our lives are as pretty as packages neatly wrapped. Some of us ignore the pain and hurt of the world, assuming it doesn't fit in this season. Others of us see the pain and imagine that it diminishes the true meaning of this season. Forgive us all, O God, for in doing these things we fail to experience fully the power of your presence among us, a presence that does not deny our pain but breaks through it to show your peace in the midst of any storm.

(DORISANNE COOPER)

ASSURANCE OF PARDON

God's love for us is stronger than anything we face. Nothing we do will ever change God's ability to break in and love us, even in the midst of our sin. In Jesus Christ, the one who was and is the presence of peace in the midst of anguish, we are forgiven.

(DORISANNE COOPER)

PASTORAL PRAYER

God our joy, we give you thanks for your gracious deeds and your praiseworthy acts. You have lifted us up and carried us through all our days. In this season of glad shouts and songs, we are truly grateful for your gentle touch and the calm of your voice. In the midst of happy echoes, we hear the cries of those who are even now in death's shadow, remembering that at your Son's birth was also heard the lamentation of Rachel weeping for her children. Be with all who grieve in this holy season and with those who are dying while others are alive with anticipation at the beginning of another year. Free us from slavery to the fear of death. Let us hear again the angel's greeting: "Do not be afraid" and live in the assurance that Jesus, who came not to a prince's cradle but to the cross, calls us sisters and brothers and shares with us all things, even our death. Grant us grace to know your promise that we will also be raised with Christ and that you will finally destroy the one who has the power of death. Lead us to your streams of living waters and bring your children to glory at last; through Jesus Christ our Lord. Amen.

(BLAIR G. MEEKS)

BENEDICTION

Live in the knowledge that the God of this season breaks through the pain of life to show the promise and reality of what true peace can be. Amen.

(DORISANNE COOPER)

READINGS

Isaiah 60:1-6

Psalm 72:1-7, 10-14

Ephesians 3:1-12

Matthew 2:1-12

Your Light Has Come

ISAIAH 60:1-6

Like Isaiah, we have shared a vision of a time when all peoples will come to worship in the Lord and to live in God's light. Surely then, all people will live together in peace. But now, long after Jesus came, the world is still torn by hatred and violent conflict. Some of the conflict is between religious groups. Some tell us that our hope that "Jesus shall reign" is "triumphalism" and that it contributes to the conflict.

Could we have misunderstood? Perhaps we need a new kind of triumphalism. Surely, all Christians should want to share their Christian faith. But would Jesus not want us first to live, teach, and serve the joyful commitment of life that is the way of love?

We would have to start with ourselves, learning to live not just out of a professed religion, but out of a costly commitment to love. We would have to learn to practice the difficult strategies of love amidst the violence and ambiguity of life in our world. And we would have to learn how to enable others to live in love. Perhaps then, "Peace will abound . . ." (Ps. 72:7) and Jesus will indeed reign.

(JAMES L. KILLEN JR.)

Called to Loving Disobedience

MATTHEW 2:1-12

One thing that stands out in this story is the disobedience of the magi. We are told very little about these figures except that in their attempt to find the child born "King of the Jews," they receive an audience with the great King Herod. In fact, it is Herod who points their search in the right direction, with instructions to come back with details. The orders are very clear. Yet after their experience with the Christ, Matthew tells us that they went "home by another road," blatantly disregarding the orders of the king. Their journey to the messiah led them to loving disobedience of even the most powerful one.

This story traditionally marks the season of Epiphany, the manifestation of Christ to the wise men. Yet, it urges us to probe deeper into the epiphanies in our own lives, and discern, like the magi, what roads God calls us to. It asks what powers we must say no to because of Christ's manifestation to us: Consumerism? War? Dissensions that fuel only anger and hatred? These things call to us today just as Herod called to the wise men long ago. Yet, as Christ becomes manifest to his modern seekers, we, too, are asked to choose different roads: selflessness, peace, and love. The story of the magi is not just a story of long ago; it is a story of today.

Looking for Perfection

MATTHEW 2:1-12

Here we are, almost a week into the new year. How many resolutions do you think have been broken already? I won't ask how many of yours you've broken.

I've pretty much given up making resolutions. I know that I never keep them, so I don't try anymore. I find them frustrating. I really do try to be better, but somehow I keep slipping. I suppose the problem is that what I want is perfection.

When I was in high school, a friend jokingly gave me a certificate that proclaimed that I was an Officially Certified Perfect Person. For years it hung on my wall and reassured me of just how accomplished I was. As I got older, I realized just how far from perfect I really was, and I finally packed the certificate away in a box somewhere.

The truth is, of course, that none of us is perfect. We try to hide our own failings. We try to be polite by not mentioning other people's imperfections—well, not much, anyway. But the reality remains: we are imperfect creatures.

The problem with looking for perfection is that sometimes we decide that we'd rather have nothing than settle for something that is less than perfect. That's what happens with my New Year's resolutions. I make plans to start exercising, go on a diet, lose twenty pounds, and get in shape. On the third day, I'm too tired to exercise, so I go out for ice cream.

Sometimes we do the same with our spiritual lives. A while back, I went to church with a friend who had just joined the congregation. After the service, another member approached my friend and invited her to come to the Women's Society later in the week. A month or two later, my friend told me she wasn't going to that church anymore because the people weren't friendly. "But didn't they invite you to the women's group?" I asked. "Sure," she replied, "I went once, and they never invited me again." Unless they were perfect, unless they extended the invitation month after month, my friend wanted no part of them.

Often we feel that way about our place in the world situation. We can't solve the problems of institutional racism, urban decay, or world hunger. If we can't handle those important things, then we won't do anything. We become so discouraged by not being able to be perfect that we give up and do nothing at all.

But is that the example God has set for us? Is that the life Christians are called to—perfection or nothing? Is that how God has acted in our world?

In the Christmas season, we celebrated the coming of God's Son. Think for a moment about the sort of time that God chose to carry out the work of salvation. It certainly was less than ideal. If our period of history seems frightening or unstable, surely the same must be said of Palestine in the time of Jesus. The little nation of Israel had been occupied by Rome. Living there was like living on the edge of a volcano. It clearly was not a time when there was peace on earth or goodwill among people.

But if God had waited for the ideal time to do something, we would never have met Jesus or known the love of the Incarnate God. If God had waited until people were rid of selfishness and greed or had said, "I will not send my Son into such a situation," if God had waited for a happier time when the Son would have been welcomed and honored, we would still be without hope. The reality is: there is no ideal time.

Today we celebrate the Epiphany. We remember the coming of the Magi to worship the Christ Child. Suppose they had demanded perfection? What if they had waited for better weather for travel or better directions to help find their goal? What if they had said, "No, a baby in a small house in an unimportant town can't be the one"? What if they had only looked for one who seemed like a king? Then they would have overlooked that unique baby and missed the Messiah.

And God's habit of using the imperfect, the less than ideal, continued. Think of the ones Jesus called to follow him, those who made up the early church. In the Epiphany season, we remember that God's self-revelation came not just to the Jews.

The Magi, the wise ones from the East, showed that Christ was the savior of *all* people. And who are those people? Who are we told will be included in God's kingdom and invited to the heavenly banquet? Matthew says both the good and the bad (Matt. 22:10). Luke lists the poor, the crippled, the lame, and the blind (Luke 14:13). Read the Acts of the Apostles and see who appears there: Jews, Samaritans, Roman soldiers, a businesswoman from Asia, a lecturer from Egypt, peddlers, fortune-tellers, tentmakers, politicians, and beggars. None of them was perfect, but God used every one of them.

If God was willing to act when the time wasn't ideal, sending a Messiah who seemed less than kingly, using people who were far from perfect, how can we keep making excuses? We have so many opportunities, if only we will take the risk. There is so much that we can do, if only we will try, instead of waiting for the ideal time or the perfect person. We may not keep all of our resolutions, but we can try again and again. We may not have perfect faith, but we can still speak a simple word of faith. We may think that the church is less than ideal, but it is still God's family. We can still come here to be fed at God's table and strengthened with God's word. We may not be able to solve the problems of the world, but we can help make our corner of it a more love-filled place.

We are not perfect, even as we begin yet another new year. We are all less than ideal. But God always uses the imperfect. God will use you, too, if you are willing.

(Catherine A. Ziel)

Prayers for Worship

Call to Worship

(Based on Isaiah 60:1-6)

Leader: Arise, shine; for your light has come!

People: And the glory of the Lord has arisen upon you.

Leader: Lift up your eyes and look around.

People: Then shall you see and be radiant.

Leader: Arise, shine; for your light has come!

People: Let us proclaim the praise of the Lord!
(CATHERINE A. ZIEL)

PRAYER OF CONFESSION

Gracious God, we are a people who dwell in darkness. We have turned from your ways to walk our own paths. We have not made the cause of the poor our own. We have not made your love known to the world in our words and our lives. We have waited for the right time and have missed our chance to act in your time. All this we bring before you now, and we ask you, in love, to speak the word of forgiveness. Amen.
(CATHERINE A. ZIEL)

ASSURANCE OF PARDON

God's love falls like showers on the grass. God's forgiveness drops on all who seek it. Jesus Christ has come to bring light in your darkness. Know that you are forgiven, and walk now in paths of righteousness.
(CATHERINE A. ZIEL)

BENEDICTION

Arise, shine; let your hearts rejoice. You are servants of the Lord according to the gift of God's grace. Be filled with the light of Christ, and go forth as bearers of that light. Arise, shine; for your light has come!
(CATHERINE A. ZIEL)

Year

B

READINGS

Isaiah 64:1-9

Psalm 80:1-7, 17-19

1 Corinthians 1:3-9

Mark 13:24-37

Let's Talk About Time

ISAIAH 64:1-9

It must have been at least a thousand years since there has been so much talk about *time*, especially with a focus on a feared end time. Historic milestones such as the approach of the new millennium found the church itself entering into its annual Advent period of waiting and anticipation with a special poignancy.

Americans, especially, are not very good at this waiting aspect of life. We are accustomed to living in an age of immediacy. Microwave ovens, photocopiers, and computers have trained us to believe that our wants and needs can be satisfied in minutes, sometimes seconds. Three months of winter can seem endless; nine months of a difficult pregnancy may seem an eternity. Desire for immediate gratification leads some down the path of drugs, sexual promiscuity, divorce, restlessness, and boredom.

How we wait and for what we wait make a difference in our experience of time. For those who wait with fear or anxiety, the test results from the doctor, a pink slip from work, or the death of a loved one, time can feel like an eternal dread. On the contrary, the excitement and anticipation of expecting a letter or a visit from a loved one, a long-desired baby, or a hard-earned graduation or promotion can make the wait as life-giving as the completed reality. Often the difference lies in a sense of hope.

Advent is, of all things, a time of hope! Early Christians were known by how they loved one another; today's Christians need to give witness to how we hope. In spite of all that calls us to despair, Christians hope because we believe in Emmanuel. We have not been left alone. Every moment of time is a gift to us to recognize and celebrate God's saving love and power at work, bringing about the fullness of God's reign. Every moment of time is an opportunity to give God glory through a loving and caring response for all creation and for each of God's creatures.

Yet hope can be a hard commodity to come by during this season where the darkness of the days often accentuates the gloom many find within. Abundant tree lights and glittering ornaments do little to relieve the depression some people feel at this time of year. And ironically, the artificial gaiety surrounding us at Christmas seems to accentuate the loneliness and emptiness in a singular way.

The people of Isaiah's time knew what it was to be living in a time of despair. In their case, despair had been brought about by their own sinfulness and forsaking of God's ways. They knew that their only path to hope lay in God's deliverance from their sinfulness and from their desperate need. Claiming their relationship with God as Abba, Father, and Mother, they cried out: "O that you would tear open the heavens and come down" (Isa. 64:1). They begged God the potter, who had first fashioned them, to forgive their iniquity and to fashion them anew.

One look at our daily newspaper or five minutes of listening to the TV news readily enables us to recognize the relevancy of the Isaiah passage for contemporary times. Can we acknowledge our sinfulness: our greed, racism, sexism, violence, power struggles, abuse of children and elderly, lack of respect for human life and for creation, alienation from one another? Can we recognize our desperation enough to let ourselves be pliable in the hands of our loving potter who can mold us, shape us anew?

But such surrender must not be interpreted as a call for a passive stance. Six times in the last four verses of today's Gospel reading, we are admonished to stay awake, be alert, watch. This very active response suggests that instead of our waiting this Advent, God is waiting for us to wake up to the truth that God has entered our history. Emmanuel, God with us, is waiting for us to recognize where God is saying yes and where God is saying no in this time and to respond to that. We are called to a state of readiness.

My sister suffered from a brain tumor for eighteen years. She had a card at her bedroom door that read, "Call me when you're ready, God, but, please God, make me ready when you call!" And ready she was as a woman who persevered in faith, in hope, in love for God, God's people, and God's creation.

Unfortunately, it is often the dying person who begins to treasure every moment of life. A few years ago, I was driving with a friend who was preparing to go to Germany to see her thirty-three-year-old sister-in-law who was dying of cancer. "I don't know what to say to her, nor to my brother who is so crazy about her," Agnes said. "I don't know what you should say, Agnes," I had to reply. "I only know that they are probably both treasuring the gift of the day. Here we are driving along; we could be killed in a car crash today. The question is, are we treasuring the gift of this day and living it fully?" The phone call came two weeks later. Agnes had been killed in a car crash in Germany on her way to visit her sister-in-law. I thought of our last conversation.

"Our lives are as brief as the hyphen between the dates on a gravestone,"[1] said David Buttrick. From God's perspective, perhaps the same is true of the time between "Christ has come" and "Christ will come again." The major question remains: Are we living the hyphen fully? Are we awake, watchful, on guard for the many ways in which our God is daily adventing into our lives, supporting us, challenging us to bring the light of God's truth and love into this world's darkness?

"O house of Jacob, come, let us walk in the light of the LORD!"

the psalmist cries (Isa. 2:5). As Christians we add, "Let us radiate for the world the light that is Christ."

Many people have lost hope. They are disillusioned, and, yes, some are despairing that things can ever be different. Cuts in government aid, cuts in medical assistance, job losses, the poor getting poorer as some CEOs' salaries reach the obscene—all cause a sense of powerlessness, a feeling of impasse. It is such experiences, however, that can move us to recognize the need for God. Only God can change the scene, and God's will is to do it in and through those who have hope.

The sense of darkness and despair leads to ennui, to inaction, to paralysis. The reality of Advent, however, is the admonition to be on guard, be awake, be alert. God has chosen to need us to make God's love, presence, compassion, and power tangible. We cannot afford to be sleepwalkers. Time is too precious; God's people are too precious! Our lives are meant to make a difference in God's world, no matter how small that difference may seem to each of us. Maranatha!

(JOAN DELAPLANE, O.P.)

Note

1. David G. Buttrick, *Preaching Jesus Christ: An Exercise in Homiletic Theology* (Philadelphia: Fortress Press, 1988), 75.

Bringing Order to Chaos

1 CORINTHIANS 1:3-9

To read these words of thanksgiving to God by Paul, in a letter in which he is about to issue strong rebuke and correction, appears to be a contradiction—particularly when we consider the situation at Corinth and a church that has abused God's love and misused God's spiritual gifts to cause division within the membership. Yet, when we pay close attention to these words of thanksgiving to God, Paul from the very beginning of this letter encourages us that, even in divisive situations within the house of God or any organization, God can and God will bring order to chaos.

This is what Paul stresses as he gives thanks to God for the Corinthian church and all of its headaches, horror stories, and problems. He thanks God because he knows that within the chaos, God has already done marvelous things that can bring blessing to the multitudes. God has done the same with us. As we approach our challenges, let us give God thanks before the blessing, and let us extend encouragement to those in the struggle. In so doing, we will plant seeds of reconciliation and bring order to chaos.

In his thanksgiving, Paul does this in three primary ways. First of all, he offers hope. In his initial approach to the Corinthian church and its chaotic problems, Paul offers hope by first extending grace and peace to every reader or hearer of the letter. It is grace and peace that are sorely missing from the Corinthian fellowship. It is grace and peace that Paul, simply by his words, seeks to reestablish in the midst of the dissension and division.

God had been very gracious to the Corinthian membership. These were people who once carried a sour reputation of being unruly and highly immoral. But they were people who had experienced the liberating power of Jesus, the Christ. They needed to be reminded of this and reminded of the peace that could pull them out from the traps of that old reputation. Every now and then, all of us need to be reminded of God's grace extended to us, so that we don't fall into old traps.

Paul offers them hope by reminding them that through grace, accompanied with the unity and love found in peace, the Corinthian church has already been enriched in every way—in all their speaking and all their knowledge. Paul reminds them that through grace they do not lack any spiritual gift. God has provided it all. Therefore, the tools for making peace and restoring order are already present within the church.

The tools for reestablishing harmony in our chaotic situations or divisive church settings are present as well. Paul reminds us that when we remind people that God's unmerited favor is available and extended to us through Jesus Christ, good can come from bad situations, even when we don't warrant it. We need to offer hope from the start to encourage others as we seek to resolve conflicts and divisions within our churches and organizations.

Second, in Paul's thanksgiving, he reminds the church that God will keep them. When we find ourselves having to address divisiveness in the ranks, we need to encourage others and be assured ourselves that God will keep us strong to the end. For conflict resolution and reconciliation in general is not easy work. There will be times when we will feel like throwing in the towel. In Paul's situation, he had a number of divisive issues disrupting harmony in the church that were taking place at the same time. From sexual immorality to the abuse of the communion ritual and the misuse and abuse of spiritual gifts, the tension Paul was called to confront was thick. But we need to know—as the apostle stresses—that God will keep us. In God we will find strength to endure.

A colleague once told me, when I was in the midst of working to reconcile a bad situation, "You can look at this as a burden or an opportunity. If you look at it as a burden, it will be just that, a burden. But if you look at it as an opportunity, then the sky's the limit as to what God can do to fix the situation."

We need to look at our challenging situations as opportunities for God's blessing. When we know that God will keep us strong to the end, we will have strength to press on through the barriers that block us from unity and love, and we will be able to bring order to chaos.

Finally, in Paul's thanksgiving, he reminds the Corinthian church (and us today) that God is faithful. For the God who has called us into fellowship with Jesus is the same God who stands ready, willing, and able to keep this fellowship sound and strong. God will do whatever is necessary to restore order out of chaos. God is faithful. The question is, will we be faithful in bringing order to the chaos? My prayer is that we will.

(*JOSEPH W. DANIELS JR.*)

Will He Find Us Ready?

MARK 13:24-37

Did you ever have the feeling that you could hardly wait until something happened, that if it didn't materialize soon you would just burst? I remember once, when I was a child, my father was away from home on what seemed to me to be an incredibly long trip. As the time drew near for his return, with the usual impatience of childhood I could hardly bear the waiting time. There were many conflicting emotions: excitement at the thought of seeing him, a great sense of love for the one who was not only father but friend, apprehension that something might happen that could delay his return, and yet, underlying everything else, the unquestioning trust of a child who knew that her father would be just as delighted to see her as she was to see him. And somehow, as we awaited his coming, life had to be lived, normal duties performed, as well as the special preparations to welcome the beloved, for maybe, just maybe, he might come earlier than we expected, and it would never do if all was not in readiness for him when he came.

As part of the cycle of the Christian year, we come again to the very special time of Advent, the word that literally means "coming," when we "remember" (put flesh again onto) the God who came to us in Jesus, when we celebrate his presence with us now, and when we look forward to the time when he will come again to bring all things to their fulfillment. Advent is essentially a waiting time, an "in-between" time, a period between two very definite events—one that has happened and one that is promised but has still to materialize. How do we, as the church, as followers and friends of Jesus, wait in this time? When you've been waiting for something for a long while, it can be difficult to continue living with expectancy. When hope begins to fade, the vision becomes blurred. When hard trials come, when we personally enter the place of dereliction, or when sometimes the whole earth seems to be covered in darkness, the sense of Advent can be anesthetized and the "in-between" becomes a no-man's-land where we drift aimlessly or fall asleep because we cannot cope. We may pray, as did the prophet of old, "Oh that you would burst from the heavens and come down—and sort everything out" (see Isa. 64:1), but our belief that this will actually ever happen, let alone that Christ might come earlier than expected, tends to be minimal or nonexistent.

I cannot help myself, but each year I approach the season of Advent with a sense of awe and wonder, as if my whole being is on tiptoe. For me it is a threshold time, a thin time, as if the veil between what we see and touch and know and the unseen world of mystery, of spiritual reality, is very fine and at any moment could be lifted. I have the sense of being surrounded by countless others from every age who are passionately waiting for the God who comes. We don't know when that will be. Neither the angels in heaven nor Jesus himself knows that; only God knows. And in a sense, it doesn't really matter. What does matter is what we do in the in-between time, in this threshold time; what matters is how we live right now. Do we wait passively or passionately? And if we're waiting passionately, then we're going to stay alert and keep watch, ready to pick up any sign of what God is doing, and to join in, to cooperate with God. If we have a passion for God, then that passion must translate itself into a resulting compassion for others, a yearning and an aching to see a world where justice and right relationships prevail, and a willingness to become makers rather than simply lovers of peace.

You know, there is a sense in which for us as Christians—as those who seek, however stumblingly, to be image bearers of Jesus— every day is Advent; every day is a *kairos* time. We are, could we but see, on the threshold of so much. God is pointing to countless doors of opportunity that God is opening for the bearers of good news, for those who will light a candle rather than curse the darkness. Not only that, God has equipped us, as Paul reminds us, with every spiritual gift we need as we eagerly await the return of Jesus. So there are no excuses for deserting the posts assigned to us, or for falling asleep, or for giving up any hope of Christ's return.

In terms of the story Jesus told, the role of the gatekeeper, the one who continually watches, is crucial. Where are the gatekeepers in the church today? I believe that they are the ones who watch in prayer, who refuse to give up but who keep on keeping on in faithful persistent prayer as they watch for his return. It is their prayer that enables the rest of us—if we have eyes to see and ears to hear—to truly be an Advent people, to perform the tasks assigned to us, as well as to make special preparations to welcome the Beloved, for maybe, just maybe, he may come earlier than we expect, and it would never do if all were not in readiness for him when he comes.

(RUTH PATTERSON)

Prayers for Worship

CALLS TO WORSHIP

(Adapted from Isaiah 9:2)

Leader: The people who walked in darkness have seen a great light;

People: Those who lived in a land of deep darkness—on them light has shined.

Leader: Come, let us worship the God

People: Whose light brings hope to a weary world.

(JOAN DELAPLANE, O.P.)

(Based on Psalm 80)

Leader: Give ear, O Shepherd of Israel, you who lead Joseph like a flock!

People: **Stir up your might, and come to save us!**

Leader: Give us life, and we will call on your name.

People: **Restore us, O LORD of hosts; let your face shine, that we may be saved.**

(RUTH PATTERSON)

(Based on Psalm 80)

Leader: Give ear, O Shepherd of Israel, you who lead Joseph like a flock! You who are enthroned upon the cherubim, shine forth. Stir up your might, and come to save us!

People: **Restore us, O God; let your face shine, that we may be saved.**

Leader: O Lord God of hosts, how long will you be angry with your people's prayers? You have fed them with the bread of tears, and given them tears to drink in full measure. You make us the scorn of our neighbors; our enemies laugh among themselves.

People: **Restore us, O God of hosts; let your face shine, that we may be saved.**

Leader: You brought a vine out of Egypt; you drove out the nations and planted it. You cleared the ground for it; it took deep root and filled the land. The mountains were covered with its shade, the mighty cedars with its branches; it sent out its branches to the sea, and its shoots to the river. Why then have you broken down its walls, so that all who pass along the way pluck its fruit?

People: **Restore us, O God of hosts; let your face shine, that we may be saved.**

Leader: Turn again, O God of hosts; look down from heaven, and see; have regard for this vine, the stock that your right hand planted. They have burned it with fire, they have cut it down; may they perish at the rebuke of your countenance. But let your hand be upon the one at your right hand, the one whom you made strong for yourself. Then we will never turn back from you; give us life, and we will call on your name.

People: **Restore us, O Lord God of hosts; let your face shine, that we may be saved.**

(SCOTT HALDEMAN)

PRAYER OF CONFESSION

Rouse your strength, O Shepherd of Israel; come and save us. We have been rebels who have resisted being clay in your loving hands. We have turned from you and sought to fashion our own lives. We have sinned. By your grace, we desire never to turn from you again. With life renewed, we shall invoke your name.

(JOAN DELAPLANE, O.P.)

(Adapted from Isaiah 40:1-2)

Leader: Comfort, O comfort my people, says your God. Speak tenderly to Jerusalem, and cry to her that she has served her term, that her penalty is paid.

People: **Thanks be to God.**

(JOAN DELAPLANE, O.P.)

(Isaiah 64:4-6, 8-9)

Leader: We have all become like one who is unclean,

People: **And all our righteous deeds are like a filthy cloth.**

Leader: We all fade like a leaf,

People: **And our iniquities, like the wind, take us away.**

Leader: Yet, O LORD, you are our Father;

People: **We are the clay, and you are our potter; we are all the work of your hand.**

Leader: Do not be exceedingly angry, O LORD,

People: **And do not remember iniquity forever.**

(RUTH PATTERSON)

PASTORAL PRAYER

O that you would tear open the heavens and come down, we pray, in the words of the prophet. We await you eagerly. We yearn for the culmination of your promised grace. And, as we wait, we struggle on. We proclaim and hear your Word; enliven your Word in our hearts that they might burn. We gather around your table to share bread; sanctify us in the meal, and multiply the loaf to feed a hungry world. We speak truth to power; overturn injustice. We shelter the homeless and provide clothes for the naked; help us to persevere. Enlighten us to cure the causes of poverty and not only its symptoms. Chasten us when we are self-righteous. Reveal how our comfort depends on the misery of others. Work in us so that you might find us blameless on that great day when you return. We are your elect, recipients of your grace; strengthen us as we work, and as we wait, so that we can stay awake and receive you. Amen.

(SCOTT HALDEMAN)

BENEDICTIONS

"May the God of hope fill you with all joy and peace in believing, so that you may abound in hope by the power of the Holy Spirit" (Rom. 15:13). Go now to be Christ's light in this world's darkness, hope for this world's despair, energy for this world's ennui.

(JOAN DELAPLANE, O.P.)

(Adapted from Mark 13)

And now go out into the world in peace. Beware, keep alert, for we do not know the hour when we will see the Son of Man coming in clouds with great power and glory. Be faithful in service and persistent in prayer; be Advent people, loving and serving the Lord. Amen.

(RUTH PATTERSON)

READINGS

Isaiah 40:1-11

Psalm 85:1-2, 8-13

2 Peter 3:8-15*a*

Mark 1:1-8

Here Is Your God!

ISAIAH 40:1-11

The prophets spoke words of judgment against ancient Israel, harsh, shrill, and wrath-filled words. Isaiah says this about Jerusalem and its inhabitants:

How the faithful city has become a whore!
　She that was full of justice, righteousness lodged in her—
　but now murderers!
Your silver has become dross, your wine is mixed with water.
Your princes are rebels and companions of thieves. (1:21-23)

But for the prophets of ancient Israel, judgment is never the final word. Condemnation is not the goal. Destruction is not the end result. The prophets mingled their words of judgment with words of hope, restoration, and comfort.

Chapter 40 of Isaiah marks the beginning of what scholars call

Second Isaiah. Most believe that the book of Isaiah is actually a compilation of prophetic writings that come from three different time periods in the life of ancient Israel: chapters 1–39 from the preexilic period (before 587); chapters 40–55 from the exilic period (587–538); and chapters 56–66 from the postexilic period (after 538). Isaiah 40, then, marks the beginning of prophetic words addressed to the Israelites who had been captured by the Babylonians in 587 and exiled to Babylon. The Babylonian Israelites were heirs to generations of Israelites who had broken their covenant with the Lord time and time again. The Lord spoke these words to the prophets during the reign of Manasseh (687–642):

> I am bringing upon Jerusalem and Judah such evil that the ears of everyone who hears of it will tingle. I will stretch over Jerusalem. . . . I will wipe Jerusalem as one wipes a dish, wiping it and turning it upside down . . . because they have done what is evil in my sight. (2 Kings 21:12-15)

The Israelites had sinned for so long and in so many ways that the words of judgment spoken by Isaiah, Jeremiah, Micah, and Habakkuk would indeed come to pass. The covenant had been broken once and for all—the Lord declared, "You are not my people and I am not your God" (Hos. 1:9). The Babylonians marched in; the presence of the Lord departed from the temple (Ezek. 10); the Babylonians destroyed Jerusalem and the temple; they deported the Israelites to Babylon. The kingdom of Judah with its God enthroned in Jerusalem was no more.

But the prophetic words do not end there. In Isaiah 40, we read words of hope for the Israelite people and for Jerusalem, the city in which God's presence had dwelled among the people. "Speak tenderly to Jerusalem, and cry to her that she has served her term, that her penalty is paid" (v. 2). And Isaiah promises that God will return to the city and dwell once again among the people.

> In the wilderness prepare the way of the LORD, make straight in the desert a highway for our God . . . say to the cities of Judah, "Here is your God!". . . He will feed his flock like a shepherd; he

will gather the lambs in his arms, and carry them in his bosom, and gently lead the mother sheep. (vv. 3, 9, 11)

Imagine the effect of these words on the Israelites in exile in Babylon, wondering if they would ever see their homeland again and if God's presence was still among them. Isaiah tells the people to carve out a processional path, make the necessary preparations, because soon they will participate in the joyous return of the Lord to Jerusalem and enthronement in the temple. They were indeed the Lord's people, and the Lord was their God.

Abraham Heschel describes Isaiah 40–55 as "prophecy tempered with human tears, mixed with a joy that heals all scars, clearing a way for understanding the future in spite of the present."[1] The people had sinned, and judgment had been carried out. There was no going back to "the way things were." But the penalty had been paid; God would begin anew with the people. Words of hope, words of comfort, words about restoration. "Lift up your voice with strength, O Jerusalem, herald of good tidings, lift it up, do not fear" (v. 9). Words of comfort to the Israelites in exile in Babylon; timeless words of hope to all generations of believers.

(NANCY L. DECLAISSÉ-WALFORD)

Note

1. Abraham Heschel, *The Prophets: An Introduction*, vol. 1 (New York: Harper & Row, 1962), 145.

It Takes Time!

2 PETER 3:8-15a

She is alone. After sixty-one years of marriage, she is alone. After the funeral, her daughter wanted to spend the night with her, but she wanted to be alone. The pastor's parting words were, "It takes time."

They are trying again. Things got so busy. Time just flew. Then two strangers stared at each other across the breakfast table. So, they are trying to rekindle the spark in their marriage. The counselor said, "You did not get into this overnight, you won't be out of it overnight. It takes time."

Cancer was the last word she wanted to hear. They said they got it all. Today, she takes the last agonizing treatment. But what is a few minutes in light of the time it could buy her? She has decided that whether she has one day or thirty-one years, she will make the best of the time she has left. Time—our most precious possession.

Peter says the time will come (v. 10). As the first-generation Christian leaders were dying off, false teachers who scoffed at the Second Coming were trying to elbow their way into the theology in process of the early church. Indeed, some like Mark (9:1) and Paul (1 Cor. 7:26, 29, 31) had said the time is short. False teachers scoffed at their sense of urgency. But Peter reminds them and us that God keeps his promises about Christ's return (v. 9). Sometimes, it just takes time.

Simon also reminds us that God's time is not necessarily our time. Quoting Psalm 94, he reiterates that a thousand years is like a day to God. When you think of it, it is pure arrogance on our part to think that God has to conform to our schedules and timetables. I mean, who invented time in the first place? Besides, God uses this time to allow others opportunity to repent (v. 9). We have had time to repent. Why shouldn't they? What is a few days of delay in light of eternity?

Peter also gives to us a word as to how we can prepare for the time! He describes the transition in such terms of radical transformation; surely we should take our preparation seriously. In fact, the false teachers had lost their sense of immediacy and had lapsed into a libertine lifestyle, but Peter points out that we should live lives that are "holy and godly" (v. 11 NIV). We should make every effort to appear before him as "spotless, blameless and at peace" when the time comes (v. 14 NIV). We should be grateful that his delay gives us and others time to prepare (v. 15).

Then he says a most astounding thing. He states that we can actually hasten the time of Jesus' coming (v. 12). Perhaps Simon recalled our Lord's statement that the preaching of the gospel to everyone would precede his coming. If we want Christ to return soon, get out and tell the story to speed the time. As Snuffy Smith says, "Time's a wastin'." It takes time. But the time is coming. In that we find hope. We find hope in Peter's wonderful assurance that the time will come when righteousness will find a home (v. 13). Somewhere, some time, things will be right.

It is that hope that sustains the small rural church to cope with dwindling resources and changing leadership. It is that hope that sustains the inner-city church to deal with the violence that surrounds it and the members fleeing to the comfortable suburbs.

The rent is due, the washer is out, and both boys need new shoes. Her former husband's check is very late, again, and like last month may not come at all. She wonders how long she can keep it up. She doesn't know about tomorrow, but for one more day, this day, she has determined to live with integrity, hope, and the refusal to sink into despair. She will live one day at a time. Things will be better. The time will come. It just takes time.

(*Gary L. Carver*)

Encounter at Kmart

Mark 1:1-8

I always wanted to meet John the Baptist, this desert wild man who lived on locusts and honey, who announced that Jesus was coming and that people had better get ready. Well, I got the chance. I met John the Baptist the other day. I met him at the Kmart.

When I drove by the corner of Glenside and Broad Streets, I looked for the man I've gotten used to seeing there. He holds a sign that reads, "I'll work for food." But this time he wasn't there.

Someone else was in his place. This new guy looked just as disheveled but quite a bit wilder in the eyes. He held a sign made out of a torn-up cardboard box. It read, "It's time for a change."

I passed within two feet of him as I turned into the parking lot. He caught my eye for a moment and held my gaze as I made the turn, almost causing a minivan pileup. But to be honest, once I was in the store I didn't think of him again.

I got my cart and combed the store for all the essentials. More clear bulbs for the window candles, a few more extension cords, Christmas-patterned paper towels. Then into the checkout line where I exchanged holiday pleasantries with other hurried shoppers while I scratched a couple of items off my "to do" list.

Before picking up my bags I reached into my wallet for some extra change. I have a personal holiday policy of never passing a Salvation Army kettle without putting something in it. I wondered if my policy was really one of generosity or if it simply helped me avoid the guilt I felt when I passed by a kettle and the collector wished me "Merry Christmas" anyway.

With packages up to my chin, a fist full of pennies, and a swoosh of the automatic doors, I was out of the building. I immediately heard the bell; but there was no kettle, only John the Baptist ringing the bell and still holding his sign, "It's time for a change." He didn't look like an official of the Salvation Army, but who am I to judge?

"Nice sign," I said. "If it's change you want I've got some right here in my hand." I thought it was witty. He was clearly not amused.

"Are you prepared?" he asked me with intimidating intensity.

"Well, not yet. That's what all these packages are about. I've got a lot of decorating to do. And my husband and I have our annual Christmas open house, and I haven't even started baking. It's more than a little overwhelming. So, I've started a list of things I simply must do to be prepared."

"Let me help you," he said. Again he held my gaze. I wondered what he could do to lighten my burden. "Let me help you take your packages to your car. Then I'll buy you a cup of coffee."

"Wait a minute. You're the one standing out in the cold with a sign. I thought I was supposed to buy you the coffee."

He didn't say a word. He just tucked his sign under his arm and unburdened me of some of my baggage. When I opened the car door, he saw one of my most-prized possessions there on the seat. He said, "Better bring that with you." So I picked up my daily planner and followed him back into the store.

There in the snack bar over a hot cup of coffee he leafed his way through my life—my lists and schedule. Most of the time, he just shook his head. Occasionally he would let out a disapproving grunt. Once he mumbled something sarcastic under his breath. I felt like a schoolgirl watching a teacher grade a test and realizing that I hadn't answered a single question correctly.

Then he brightened up. "O.K. Here's something I like," he finally said. " 'Get rid of clutter. Clear a path.' Tell me about that."

I explained that my den was strewn with boxes of Christmas decorations that had been hiding in my garage since we had moved in that summer. I needed time to sort out the Santa place mats from the nativity scenes and to clear a path through my den.

His shoulders fell with disappointment, and he went back to his review. When he had finished reading, he turned to a new page in my planner. Then he reached in his pocket and pulled out an old pencil stub. It was the kind you use to keep score in miniature golf, and it was worn down to half its size but freshly sharpened as if prepared for this moment. He smoothed the paper, being sure to flatten any bends, wrinkles, or raised places. He then touched the tip of his pencil to his tongue and wrote for me a new list. I watched in silence as this vagabond in the suburban wilderness wrote intently on the pages of my priorities.

At the top of the page he wrote, "DO LIST." Number 1 said, "Hold a baby." What a strange instruction. Before I could ask him to explain I heard a woman next to me let out a squeal. Her toddler had climbed up a display to get a closer look at a stuffed Tickle-Me-Something-or-Other. The display began to teeter.

Without a word between us, she passed me her newborn to hold as she ran after her little climber.

I looked down at the bundle she had placed in my arms. He was so tiny, so fragile. He reached for my face with his delicate hand. The store's sound system played an instrumental version of "What Child Is This," and for a moment I wasn't in Kmart but in Bethlehem. I was holding close to me the tiny body of the one whose body would be broken for me. The tiny hand reaching for me was the hand that would reach out to embrace the cosmos and then bear a nail on my behalf.

Too soon an announcement of a "blue-light special" broke into the moment, and the mother returned for her baby. I glanced back at my planner and saw Number 2: "Wonder." Wonder? Wonder what? Wonder why God chose a helpless little baby to bring salvation into a hostile world? Wonder why after thousands of years we still haven't gotten the message? Wonder when Christ will come again? I wondered. I wondered what to wonder. And I wondered some more.

The announcement came over the loudspeaker. The store was closing. Bring final purchases to the register. Where had the time gone? How long had I been sitting there? I looked around but didn't see John anywhere. I glanced down at the third item on my DO LIST. "Look to the stars." What did that mean?

As I walked outside, I heard a plane overhead. I looked up to see a clear sky full of stars. There were thousands of them. More beautiful than the lights on any Christmas tree. They took my breath. And I hadn't had to work to put them up there. I hadn't had to untangle the cords or check for dud star-bulbs. This light display required no extension cord. It was placed there for me as a gift, an unmerited spectacle of wonder.

There in the parking lot, looking into the night sky, I had a strong sense that I had been looking in the wrong place for Christmas. I had been too busy rushing around to look up. I had been so busy worrying about what I had to do that I forgot to appreciate what had already been done for me. I had been so preoccupied with following the crowd that I had neglected to follow the star.

As I gazed into the sky it seemed that one star was shining a little brighter than all the rest. Remembering the stranger's admonition I followed it. Perhaps it would lead me to Bethlehem. As I walked through the cold night, to my amazement, the light of the star seemed to fall upon my minivan. In the starlight I could just see the cardboard sign, tucked under my windshield wiper. "It's time for a change," the sign reminded me.

No matter how your Advent season is going so far, it is not too late. It is not too late to hold a child, to wonder, to look up, to follow a star. It's not too late for a change. Take it from me. I know it for a fact. I learned it the night I met John the Baptist at the Kmart.

(Rhonda VanDyke Colby)

Prayers for Worship

Calls to Worship

(Based on Psalm 85)

Leader: LORD, you were favorable to your land; you restored the fortunes of Jacob.

People: You forgave the iniquity of your people; you pardoned all their sin.

Leader: You withdrew all your wrath; you turned from your hot anger.

People: Restore us again, O God of our salvation, and put away your indignation toward us.

Leader: Show us your steadfast love, O Lord, and grant us your salvation. Let me hear what God declares, for he will speak peace to his people, to his faithful, to those who turn to him in their hearts.

People: **Show us your steadfast love, O Lord, and grant us your salvation.**

(SCOTT HALDEMAN)

One: In this season of mystery,

Many: **Let us watch for God's surprises!**

One: Steadfast love and faithfulness will meet; righteousness and peace will kiss each other.

Many: **The ordinary will encounter the extraordinary.**

One: And something . . .

Many: **Something extraordinary will happen.**

One: Watch!

(RHONDA VANDYKE COLBY)

PRAYER OF CONFESSION

O Surprising One, we confess that we continually look for you in the ordinary places: on the front of Christmas cards, in the plastic nativity scenes on our neighbors' lawns, in familiar carols, in the church we call home. We watch for the blanketed babe with the omniscient smile and the heavenly glow. So sure are we of how you will appear to us that we miss your incarnation where we do not expect it. We have failed to see you enfleshed in our enemies. We have not recognized you in faces that do not look like our own in their color and shape and age. We confess that we have refused to acknowledge your incarnation in ourselves for fear that to have Christ in us would be too costly.

Forgive our narrowness. Help us to watch. Teach us to recognize. Surprise us even today, even this hour, by breaking into the ordinariness of our worship so that we might see you anew. O come, O come, Emmanuel.

(<small>RHONDA VANDYKE COLBY</small>)

ASSURANCE OF PARDON

Hear the good news! Christ is coming! With or without our recognition, God is becoming flesh. Even when we see no need for God, God sees our need and comes—again and again. Thanks be to God!

(<small>RHONDA VANDYKE COLBY</small>)

PASTORAL PRAYER

Holy Comforter, who gathered your exiled children under your wings and brought them home, shelter us this day. Speak to us tenderly of your promises. Speak words of assurance to those who doubt. Comfort your people. Speak words of healing to those who are ill. Comfort your people. Speak words of hope to those who despair. Comfort your people. Speak words of power to those who are abused and downtrodden. Comfort your people. Send once more prophets like John. Call us to repent. Call us to attend to the One who is coming. We ready ourselves for the new heaven and the new earth. Send the Spirit to baptize. Send the Spirit to transform. Send the Spirit to renew. Enliven your church. Humble the proud. Enfold the suffering. Feed the hungry. Comfort your people. Prepare us for the day of your coming. In the name of the One who shared our deepestsuffering and who was raised to live with you where suffering is no more. Amen.

(<small>SCOTT HALDEMAN</small>)

BENEDICTION

Stay awake!
   Look out!
      Look up!
         Look in!
            And wonder.

(RHONDA VANDYKE COLBY)

READINGS

Isaiah 61:1-4, 8-11

Psalm 126

1 Thessalonians 5:16-24

John 1:6-8, 19-28

Overcoming Oppressive Theology

ISAIAH 61:1-4, 8-11

Theos/logos, "God words" or words about God, are not etched in granite; they metamorphose with time. All of us see things a bit differently than we saw them ten years ago, and certainly our theology has progressed since we first met Jesus.

Some of us are "meeting Jesus again for the first time"—the title of a book I read by Marcus J. Borg.[1] We met Jesus at an earlier time, before we experienced much of life, and we thought we knew all about him—only to find out that this walk with Jesus must be experiential. You must walk with Jesus to know Jesus. And as we walk his way of suffering, our theology changes.

The church of Jesus Christ is also in the midst of change, some of it for the better, and some of it for the worse. Some of our theology binds, while some sets free.

Our Old Testament reading from Isaiah 61 reminds us of the purposes for which Jesus came. Jesus, in inaugurating his own ministry here on earth, read from this very same portion of Isaiah's scroll in the synagogue one Sabbath morning. He said the spirit of the sovereign God was upon him for these purposes:

- to preach good tidings to the meek;
- to bind up the brokenhearted;
- to proclaim liberty to the captives;
- to open the prisons of them that are bound;
- to proclaim the acceptable year—the year of Jubilee.

During this season of Advent, we must remind ourselves of the purposes for which Christ came, for these must also be our purposes. All ministry that purports to proclaim the good news of Jesus Christ must pass this litmus test: Does the ministry promote us, our views, our philosophy and dogma, or does it represent the real Jesus?

Certainly there is oppressive theology being preached in the body of Christ. Listen carefully to the television, the radio; read carefully the books and the mail. You will see three distinct basic teachings that are at the root of oppressive theology.

I. Nationality of God

In this country we often hear that "God is the God of our nation. We are the people God loves most. Let's get America back to God." It is as though we have exclusive rights to God. Indeed, in our nation, what is called Christianity is often Americanism. "God must prefer my country because I do." With this type of thinking, the majority race can close the borders, oppress minorities, or justify foreign wars because "God is our God and prefers us."

The political parties think God belongs to them. White folk think God belongs to them. Israelis think they own God; Arabs try to own God. And we African Americans sometimes feel God loves us much more than anyone else (at least more than anyone who is different from us).

Denominations, too, take on this mentality. Within the Christian church alone we teach baptism in Jesus' name, in the name of the Trinity, for adults only, for children only, by immersion, by sprinkling, as necessary for salvation, and as a prerequisite for the gift of the Holy Ghost. Each denomination feels that it has *the* revelation of God, and therefore, "If I am right, you must be wrong." Turf wars abound for ownership of the real word of God. And it is amazing the divisions these wars cause.

Yet our God is not a God of any one nation, nor of any one denomination. Nations are formed to facilitate the needs of their citizens. Denominations are set up to facilitate the work of the church on earth. Human beings, not buildings or organizations, are called to be a habitation for the Spirit of God. Therefore, we must preach a gospel that heals and brings wholeness to the person.

Is the gospel intended to imprison people to a nation or to a denomination? Isaiah preached liberty to the captives and freedom to those in bondage. This is the gospel.

II. Preconceived Interpretation

Another theology that oppresses is the theology that is born out of our own preconceived interpretations of the Bible. Often we go to the Bible already sure we know what it says. We have decided God is for this and against that, and we approach the scriptures looking for those passages that defend our own positions. It doesn't matter whether we take passages out of context or not. All that is important is defending our own point of view.

What would happen if we took a different approach to biblical study? If we came to the study of scripture seeking to understand the times, the context, the politics, the culture, the religion, and the social norms represented by thousands of years of history in the word? Then we would be better equipped to make the scriptures relevant to the times in which we live rather than having them simply feed our own biases and prejudices. Rightly divining the truth would help us know what was intended for literal translation and what was given to teach a spiritual principle.

The good news spoken by the prophet Isaiah supports a

guiding principle for our interpretation. Good interpretation, good theology, brings joy, gives comfort, and produces righteousness.

III. Inherited Oppression

And last, to my sisters and brothers of the African diaspora: We have been a historically oppressed people. We were taught the word of God by good religious folk who could sing "Amazing Grace" on the deck of a slave ship—the same people who felt fully justified by that word to sell us, brand us, beat us, and sell off our children. Our understanding of a God that could allow such atrocities would have to leave us feeling inferior.

And how does an inferior group of people feel superior? The oppressed become oppressors. It is a learned behavior. Light-colored folk feel superior to dark folk. Skinny folk feel superior to fat folk. Educated folk feel superior to undereducated folk. Men lord over women, "haves" lord over the "have-nots." The pulpit becomes a place of monarchy, not ministry. And African Americans who got their opportunity through affirmative action are now speaking against it.

The truth of the matter is this: We will not be truly free until we adopt a theology that does not oppress anyone. Oppressive theology is a chain upon our hearts, and with it we have also kept one another in chains.

So let us heed the words of the prophet Isaiah and of Jesus. Let's have a year of Jubilee! Let's lift the clouds of judgment and allow a celebration of diversity to shine forth. Let's tear down the walls of partition and loose the Spirit of God to flow from church to temple to cathedral to mission to prayer group. Let's open the prisons of those that are bound. Let's set each other free.

(*YVETTE FLUNDER AND VALERIE BROWN-TROUTT*)

Note

1. Marcus J. Borg, *Meeting Jesus Again for the First Time: The Historical Jesus and the Heart of Contemporary Faith* (San Francisco: HarperCollins, 1994).

Paul's Last-Minute Instructions

1 THESSALONIANS 5:16-24

Reading this pericope reminds me of saying good-bye to my son at the door before he leaves for school each morning. At the door, or somewhere in close proximity to the door, we go through the mother-son ritual of parting. It is a mother thing, I know that. But it has to be done. It goes something like this: "Don't forget the lunch box. Have you got all of your homework? Be sure and enjoy the day. Be safe. Have you got your gloves?" On different mornings, different adaptations of the door litany occur. When I have noticed that there was discouragement the night before or anxiety before a final examination, the words might be "hang in there until TGIF" (Thank Goodness It's Friday—where we rent a family movie and eat pizza), or "make sure you find something to smile about today."

Like the mother who wishes she had more time to have conversation with the son, she settles for these short, proverbial, morning snippets, which she hopes will be remembered sometime during the day. And as he rushes out the door and leaves her presence, she shares these loving imperatives—the kind of domestic slogans that can be imprinted in cross-stitch floss and hung on the wall in the family room.

Here at the end of Paul's letter, the situation is not that different from the mother saying good-bye to her child at the door as he leaves for school. The final words that Paul offers this beloved congregation come from his heart and his close relationship with them. The instruction has been given in the months before as he had spent time with them, worshiping and teaching in their community of faith (Acts 17). The relationship continues through the ministry of letter writing. After hearing Timothy's report, Paul writes a letter placing on paper all the words of encouragement and teaching that he has wanted to tell them since his departure. And now, at the end of the letter, anything that has been previously omitted enters the text. Those last-minute instructions that some-how did not surface in the carefully written paragraphs of episto-lary convention become piled high at the end of the letter. With love for these people Paul says to them: "Rejoice always." "Pray without ceasing." "Give thanks in all things." "Do not quench the Spirit." "Do not despise prophecy." "Test everything; hold fast to that which is beautiful." "Keep away from every kind of evil."

The pastoral (maternal) response of Paul is striking. The time is too short for long paragraphs; narrative text is too cumber-some. Short proverbial statements with an aphoristic ring fit the farewell setting.

Max Ehrmann in 1927 penned the words to "Desiderata," whose form and content are similar to Paul's own words:

> Go placidly amid the noise and haste and remember what peace there may be in silence. As far as possible without surrender be on good terms with all persons. Speak your truth quietly and clearly; and listen to others, even the full and ignorant; they too have their story. . . . Be yourself. Especially, do not feign affection. . . . Take kindly the counsel of the years, gracefully surrendering the things of youth. . . . With all its sham, drudgery and broken dreams, it is still a beautiful world. Be careful. Strive to be happy.

Paul has loved this community of faith, like a mother nursing her children (2:7), as a father teaching them (2:11). When he is not with them, he feels as if he is an orphan (2:17). His words have encouraged the new converts to have hope in the coming of Christ. And perhaps most important, his words have given them comfort as they grieved the deaths of their dear loved ones. For Paul, the most important point was not the date or time of Jesus' return, not even the specific details attached to Jesus' arrival. The significance for Paul and the community of faith was that they would be with their loved ones and with Jesus at the time of Jesus' return. Relationships were the most important element of the faith.

Relationship between the dead ones, the living ones, and the One who had come once already and would come again soon would be Paul's primary word to this community. Ethical imperatives would not be dismissed as unessential, but absolutely crucial to the well-being of the community (4:1-12). Doctrinal issues were not ignored, but made subservient to the formation of the community (4:13–5:11).

Paul's benediction, offered as a conclusion to the letter, reinforces the sense of oneness within the body of believers: "May the God of peace, God's self, sanctify you completely, even the whole of you, and may your spirit and soul and body be kept without blame in the coming of our Lord Jesus" (5:23). So be it for all of us!

(LINDA MCKINNISH BRIDGES)

Something's Coming
JOHN 1:6-8, 19-28

In the musical *West Side Story*, Tony, the lead male character, is reluctantly persuaded by his friends to come back to a world he had left, to the Jets, a New York City street gang. Although hesitant at first, his enthusiasm for the venture builds. In the excitement of being among old friends and in anticipation of new adventures that lie ahead, he sings a song entitled "Something's Coming."

As we move deeper into the experience of Advent, the Scripture readings call us to enter into a posture of joyful anticipation. Like the character in the musical, our excitement is building, but unlike him, we are not asked to return to the familiar world of our past, but to enter into a new place, a place of hope and expectation. "Something's coming," Advent tells us; it's time to get ready.

All four Gospel writers mention John the Baptist, but in the Fourth Gospel the evangelist is explicit in telling us that John's role was simply to witness, to tell the "truth, the whole truth, and nothing but the truth, so help him God" about Jesus. John the Baptist, the evangelist tells us, had a firm grasp of who he was and who he was not. John was a great man of God, but he was not God's love note to humankind, enfleshed in human form. John had a simple task—to help people get ready for the reality of God's salvation.

John was the "voice crying in the wilderness." The wilderness is an evocative image in the Scriptures. It is the "wild place" where the children of Israel learned what it meant to be the people of God. For forty years, the remaining life span of the Egypt-born generation, the children of Israel learned what it meant to listen, to follow, and to depend on the Lord. Their identity as the people of God was forged in the challenges and struggles of the wilderness. To hear the prophetic call of John involved both a literal and a figurative return to the wilderness, to the place of spiritual formation, to a place of divine encounter, to holy ground.

John's message was a simple one, so simple that the religious establishment had to send an official delegation to make sure they had heard it right. John simply said that God's salvation had come. "Who knows?" Tony sings in the musical, "I got a feeling there's a miracle due."

The Baptizer agrees. The miracle is due; in fact, John says, it is already here among us. The Light of the world stands in our midst. Following John's lead, we know two things: the miracle is not us, but with a wilderness perspective we can point to who it is. We too are witnesses to this wonder.

What a miracle it is! The One for whom we wait already stands among us in the person of Jesus. In taking a human body, once again he has blessed our humanity and given tangible form to God's reconciling love. In the words of Isaiah 61:9, we are truly the people whom the Lord has blessed. We are blessed by God's presence, by God's intervention in our lives, by God's grace and love lavished upon us, poured out on people who often fail to recognize it.

For John tells us that the One for whom we wait stands

unrecognized in our midst. He often appears in unexpected places and acts in surprising, unexpected ways. If we're not careful, we run the risk of overlooking him. We need to improve our vision, our recognition quotient. The question becomes, What are the things that prevent us from recognizing this miracle? Do we need to slow down? Do we need to remember to look for it? Do we need to take on an attitude of joy and anticipation? What are the things that need to be "made straight"—straightened out—in our lives? The Epistle reading for today gives us clues. We are called to live in a state of intimacy and communion with God, to do that which is good and avoid what is evil. That which keeps us from doing such things is to be removed so our access to God may be unhindered.

We may have some straightening out to do, but there is genuine good news! Whatever else we need to do, we need to recognize that the wilderness of our lives, that place marked by human celebration and mourning, challenge and testing, is also a place of holy encounter—holy ground. The "wild place" we inhabit on a daily basis is a habitation of the Extraordinary. We have not been abandoned. We don't have to wait until some future date to experience the miracle of God's grace.

Tony continues to sing: "And something great is coming!" Stephen Sondheim's lyrics from *West Side Story* capture the Advent spirit. Indeed, something wonderful, something beyond our wildest expectation is coming. It is right around the corner. God has spoken a Word of love, made it tangible, and set it in our midst. It is an incarnate, an enfleshed word of justice, mercy, and restoration.

"Who knows?" Tony sings, "Maybe tonight. . . ." The message of the Baptist is "maybe today!" And that is a message worth returning to the wilderness to hear; that is a message worth proclaiming. Let us rejoice and give thanks!

(VICKI G. LUMPKIN)

Prayers for Worship

CALLS TO WORSHIP

(Based on Psalm 126)

Leader: When the Lord restored the fortunes of Zion, our mouths were filled with laughter, and our tongues shouted with joy.

People: The Lord has done great things for us.

Leader: The Lord has done great things for us, and we rejoiced. Restore our fortunes, O LORD, like the watercourses in the Negeb. May those who sow in tears reap with shouts of joy.

People: The Lord has done great things for us.

Leader: Those who go out weeping, bearing the seed for sowing, shall come home with shouts of joy, carrying their sheaves.

People: The Lord has done great things for us. Let us worship God.

(SCOTT HALDEMAN)

(Based on Isaiah 61:8-11)

Leader: Let us rejoice in the Lord!

All: Let us relish God's presence wholeheartedly!

Leader: For God has adorned us with salvation's finery,

All: **and bedecked us in garments of righteousness.**

Leader: We are the people whom God has blessed.

All: **God's mercy will cause praise to spring up like flowers;**

Leader: God's justice will produce a crop of righteousness.

All: **Let us rejoice in the Lord!**

(VICKI G. LUMPKIN)

Lord of liberty and love,
We know you hate oppression of all kinds.
We seek to reflect you in the earth.
Cleanse us from our unrighteousness.
Direct our work in truth according to your word.

Lord, we seek to live our lives in covenant with you.
We seek to be seeds of blessing for your glory everywhere we
    are.
In our homes, make us a blessing.
In our neighborhoods, make us a blessing.
In our communities, make us a blessing.
Among the nations of the world, make us a blessing.

We pray that all those who see us will acknowledge
that we are the seeds that the Lord has used to bring blessing. Amen.

(YVETTE FLUNDER AND VALERIE BROWN-TROUTT)

PRAYER OF CONFESSION

(Based on 1 Thessalonians 5:16-24)

Reconciling Lord, we confess that we often are not people of prayer. We fail to seek opportunities to give thanks in the varied circumstances of our lives. We do not cling to that which is good or refrain from that which is evil. We need your sanctifying mercy. Cleanse us and ready our hearts for a deeper experience of your indwelling presence. We ask these things in the name of the One who stands among us. Amen.

(VICKI G. LUMPKIN)

ASSURANCE OF PARDON

Leader: Our assurance of pardon is found in the words of the apostle Paul: "The one who calls you is faithful, and God will do this."

All: **Thanks be to God, through Christ we are forgiven.**

(VICKI G. LUMPKIN)

PASTORAL PRAYER

Giver of all good gifts, who blesses us each day with your grace, with your Spirit, with your compassion, may your light shine in your world this day. Bind all broken hearts. Comfort those who mourn. Turn our ashes into garlands. Change our funeral suits to festival garments. Source of Mercy, sanctify us. Keep our bodies sound. Make us blameless in your sight. Spirit of the Prophets, descend on us. Make us your instruments. To visit those who are ill. To embrace the dying. To tell of your love. To work for your justice. To set free the imprisoned. To prepare your way. To cry in the wilderness—the wilderness of despair, the wilderness of pain, the wilderness of hunger, the wilderness of rejection, the wilderness of our lives. To prepare a way for you in this wilderness. Come, we prepare for you. Come, we pray. Amen.

(SCOTT HALDEMAN)

BENEDICTIONS

As you leave, my sisters and brothers,
  go greatly rejoicing in the Lord.
As you leave, my sisters and brothers,
  go clothed in the garments of salvation.
As you leave, my sisters and brothers,
  go robed in God's robe of righteousness.
As you leave, my sisters and brothers,
  go adorned with love for all people.
As you leave, my sisters and brothers,
  go living your lives so that righteousness and praise
    spring forth among all the nations. Amen.

(*Yvette Flunder and Valerie Brown-Troutt*)

Depart with an Advent hope:
Messiah is coming, Christ is with us!
May the Lord of light
illumine your way,
chase away your darkness, and
by his presence transform your wilderness
into a garden of peace, liberty, and joy.
Amen.

(*Vicki G. Lumpkin*)

READINGS

2 Samuel 7:1-11, 16

Luke 1:47-55 or Psalm 89:1-4, 19-26

Romans 16:25-27

Luke 1:26-38

The God Who Camps Out

2 SAMUEL 7:1-11, 16

Are you the one to build me a house to live in? I have not lived in a house since the day I brought up the people of Israel from Egypt to this day, but I have been moving about in a tent and a tabernacle. (2 Samuel 7:5-6)

Christmas in the Northern Hemisphere is an odd time to think about camping, but the wonderful serendipity of the texts for today carries this communiqué: This God *likes* living in a tent.

Having experienced countless more than a hundred and one wilderness nights, I've had ample time to ponder what that might mean. In a tent beside a lost lake one night, you lie wakeful, knowing that you are miles from anyone who would notice if you didn't return. The night sweats take hold of you, as you fantasize that a sudden noise or flash of lightning startles a moose out in the bush and that moose stampedes blindly into the clearing, trampling you—tent and all—in its frantic wake. Just then the forest rumbles and real hoofbeats gallop by.

Another summer night, the ground under you moans distantly, and nine months later the mountain explodes not two miles from where you'd laid your ear.

Yet another summer, beside another lake, you hear quiet snuffling three inches away, on the other side of the thin nylon wall.

And at 2 A.M. in mid-July somewhere near the Arctic Circle, you open your eyes because the back of your eyelids, and the tent itself, are alight with the sun. Constant reminders all: in a tent, you have only a membrane for protection (which is no defense at all). The startling news of Advent is that this is what God prefers, even longs for—not to be walled away from the world but to experience unprotected the nuances of weather and light and risk.

And so it is easy to understand why this God can't stand to have windows closed, cannot abide hermetically sealed spirits, chooses not to reside permanently among any tribes, even (or especially) those who think themselves divinely ordained. "Would you build me a house to live in?"

This freely moving One came into Mary's carefully planned, socially delineated life with an upheaval that she could never have expected. She was a girl properly engaged—all events in her young existence following their appropriate, prescribed trajectory—until this. And here was a God who would rather be with those who don't expect him.

What is it about Mary that makes her an appropriate object of God's grace? The text does not tell us; she is identified simply as a young girl engaged to be married. Luke reveals more about Zechariah and Elizabeth, describing them as living righteous and blameless lives. Mary, however, doesn't seem to earn or deserve the honor of a visitation more than anyone else. But recognizing this to be God's plan, not her own, she gives her consent: "Let it be with me according to your word."

As Samuel's narrative depicts it, when David resolves to perform a monumental act of piety and erect a mighty temple for Yahweh, his idea meets with divine demolition by the God who doesn't want or need a temple. This "free, mobile, dynamic God—sojourns, bivouacs, and comes and goes, but never settles and becomes confined in one place."[1]

David had hoped to build Yahweh a temple, but Yahweh turns the tables and promises to make David "a house"—a dynasty that finds its ultimate, unexpected fruition in the willingness of Mary's incarnational, Advent faith.

With all the forest sounds surrounding me that distant night, I lay in terror of my imagined moose stampede, but I would not for all the world give up hearing those ghostly beautiful hoofbeats race past me, out of darkness and away into darkness. The moment will stay with me for the rest of my life, along with a dream that followed: I was in the presence of a friend and teacher, in a log cabin somewhere, and we were laughing and singing to each other. Suddenly I stopped in midstanza and said, "I love you!" She put her arm across my shoulders—so tangibly that I woke up, convinced she had really been next to me. In that waking, I realized through and through that the night's earlier terror was gone. I was at home as a nomad, at home in this wilderness place. Was it "only a dream"?

The membrane of a tent, if we have courage to inhabit it, is too thin to protect us. But perhaps Christ enters human flesh as a way of putting his arm around our shoulders and making us at home in this frail tent that he honors, if we concur with the will that would make it his dwelling. May Jesus the Christ abide in our tents, now and all our days.

(GAIL ANDERSON RICCIUTI)

Note

1. Walter Brueggemann, in *Texts for Preaching: A Lectionary Commentary Based on the NRSV-Year B*, ed. Walter Brueggemann, et al. (Louisville: Westminster John Knox Press, 1993), 32.

The Power of a Final Praise

ROMANS 16:25-27

This concluding doxology, bringing to a close what many believe is the foundational writing of Christian theology, does not receive much respect in various circles of Christian thought. For on the one hand, a number of scholars state that the appearance of a doxology or a final praise is uncharacteristic of Paul's writings. Paul usually closed his writings with a benediction. While on the other hand, other scholars have struggled with the mechanics of these concluding words. Some say that the combination of phrases already used in the letter such as "will establish you" (1:11) and "my gospel" (2:16), with others reminiscent of the Pastoral Epistles, make it questionable that Paul even wrote this doxology. Still others suggest that these final reflections of this great apostle are out of place and should appear after chapter 14, verse 23.

But in spite of the questions and concerns that arise from the theological analysis of the text, none of these comments can dampen the fire that comes from this most powerful ending to a life-transforming letter. For if we take this final praise at face value, one thing still remains clear: God is worthy to be praised! And the apostle took time before he put his pen back in the ink jar to say so.

After all that God has done to save the world from its sin and lead us back into harmonious relationship with our Creator, Paul reminds us that we need to pause before it is all said and done to give God praise. For there is power in the praise.

There is a well-known saying that goes, "When the praises go up, the blessings come down." Well if we look at this final praise carefully, then we're left to take away from an already powerful letter great blessings to encourage us along the way.

As we look at this final praise, there is the encouragement of knowing that our God is able. The fact that God is able brings to the believer a glimmer of light in a sometimes dark world. All by itself, this fact enables us to fear no evil, even as we walk through valleys lined with death shadows.

Our God is able to see us through any danger, toil, and snare. Our God is able to heal our relationships, and fix our fractured families. Our God is able to restore peace in our communities, as well as peace throughout the world. Our God is able to bring order to our finances and healing to our tired, aching bodies. As Paul said in a moment of praise to God in his letter to the church at Ephesus, our God "is able to do immeasurably more than all we ask or imagine" (Eph. 3:2 NIV). When we realize in our hearts that God is able, we have a hope that exceeds all detrimental experiences in life. Our God is able! That's a blessing.

But then there is the assurance of knowing that our God can and will establish us and strengthen us in the good news of Jesus Christ. The "my gospel" Paul refers to is that gospel or good news of Jesus Christ that Paul in chapter 1 said he's not ashamed of. For it is the power of God for the salvation of everyone who believes.

It is personal to Paul, this gospel. Not only has he heard it with his ears, but he has seen God personally intervene in his trials to deliver him time and again. The gospel has strengthened him. When we encounter the Lord in our hardships and sufferings and experience God giving us the help and the strength to overcome all obstacles, barriers, and evil attempts to prevent us from being whole, then we, like Paul, will be compelled to give thanks and praise to the God who is worthy to be praised. For we've been blessed. And the redeemed of the Lord must say so.

But finally, in this final praise to a powerful letter, there is the blessing of knowing that God will travel to whatever depths God must go to save us. For as the apostle declares, God went as far as to sacrifice God's only Son for our salvation and the salvation of the world. Then God made this fact known to us, a fact that for so long was kept secret but now is made known through the prophetic writings. And so if God went as far as giving his Son in death to save us, surely he will go to the root of our addictions, the root of our pains, the root of our past sins and shames to deliver us. In the name of Jesus, God saves. In the name of Jesus, God heals. In the name of Jesus, God reconciles. When, like Paul, we allow God to become real in our souls, we can't help but believe and obey. And then we must say, Hallelujah! Thank you, Jesus! Through our mouths, yet through our actions, it is the only response we have to offer.

It is to this God, the only wise God, that glory and honor and praise are so richly deserving. To this God we give a final praise! Amen.

(JOSEPH W. DANIELS JR.)

Here Am I

LUKE 1:26-38

Let me be honest. As a Protestant woman, I am completely fascinated with Mary. Or maybe it would be more accurate to say that I am completely fascinated by the attention she gets from our Roman Catholic and Eastern Orthodox friends. That there is a complete liturgical tradition and culture devoted to Mary, a tradition in which I have no part and of which I am largely ignorant, sometimes makes me feel like the child of immigrants: I know my parents used to speak that language and follow those customs, but they don't make sense for me, here, in the new world. And that was surely the goal of the Reformers, wasn't it?—to so thoroughly eliminate every trace of Mary from word and sacrament that before long, people would not remember the old practices and would not be able to hand them down to their children. It only takes a generation or two of neglect, after all, to lose a culture. Sometimes that's how I feel: as if I've lost a culture that might have nourished me in ways I can't even imagine.

To be fair, I am Protestant enough that I can sympathize with some of the Reformers' original complaints about Mary and the intercession of saints. At the time of the Reformation, people often prayed to God not directly but through a saint who might petition on their behalf, and the Queen of Heaven was a clear favorite. The Reformers, mincing no words, thought this sheer stupidity; Calvin called it a "horrid sacrilege" to call upon any intermediary but Christ.[1] So the sanctuaries were stripped of all decoration, the liturgy rewritten, and the prayers simplified into forms we would immediately recognize today. In the process, Mary lost her throne. All that remains of her in our tradition is what we read in scripture.

And what is that, exactly? Who is this young woman from Nazareth who one day, out of the blue, finds herself addressed by God? Whose very proper engagement is suddenly shrouded in scandal? Whose quiet certainty convinces her fiancé not to dismiss her but to stand by her and raise the child he did not father? Whose acceptance of God's plan for her life fills her with a vision for all creation that pours out of her in song? Who is she?

In many ways, that's an impossible question. Mary is what we make of her, and that includes both good and bad. She can be the shining example of human obedience or the stunning example of blind obedience. She can be a model of courage to inspire all people or a model of passivity to keep women down. She can be the best metaphor we have for the way God enters our messy human lives, or she can be the woman on the pedestal whose purity has to be protected at all costs, even the cost of her humanness. Mary is and has been all these things. She is nothing short of an icon.

An icon. That's a word that conjures up images of the second commandment and idol worship. Protestants tend to be wary of icons. We don't use them and therefore don't understand them. They are part of our immigrant past. But what have we lost in giving up that past? How can Mary be an icon who transcends all our stereotypes?

In the harbor of Gloucester, Massachusetts, there is a Roman Catholic church called Our Lady of the Seas. The steeple bears a statue of Mary, looking out to sea, with a fishing boat cradled in her hands. It is an image of tremendous power for this community because Gloucester is a fishing village, and in its three-hundred-year history, more than thirty thousand fisherman—many of them Portuguese and Italian immigrants—have lost their lives at sea. Even today, fishing remains one of the most dangerous occupations and one of the poorest. When the storms come and the radios give out, there is nothing to do but pray. For generations, fishing wives have gone to the church to pray for their husbands' safety, and fishermen have carried the statue down to the harbor for the annual blessing of the fleet. Mary, Our Lady of the Seas. She offers no miracles. She can only cradle the boat as it puts to sea, as she once cradled her baby who was destined to die. In her strength, her resolve, the community finds its own.

The Mary we read about in scripture is the same Mary who stands watch over the Gloucester Harbor. At least I hope she is, because if the story of the annunciation is to mean anything to us, it must *announce,* today, to the fishermen of Gloucester, that God in Christ has defeated the powers of this world. It must announce, today, to migrant workers in Texas, that God in Christ has brought down the mighty from their thrones. It must announce, today, to Asian women forced into prostitution that God in Christ has lifted up the lowly. Our Lady of the Seas, Our Lady of the Fields, Our Lady of the Brothels—it is the same Mary, the same peasant girl who heard the angel, and accepted the news, and set her face toward a future in God's hands.

We do not need to keep her pure. The story tells us that she left pure behind. She left safe behind. She left proper and comfortable and secure far behind her and traded them for a vision of God incarnate in every single human life, no matter how poor or dirty or lost at sea. The Mary we read about in scripture is not on some pedestal, but on a steeple, watching the fleet as it leaves the harbor. And the prayer on her lips is anything but meek; it is joyful anticipation, uttered through tears and gritted teeth, of the day when every soul shall magnify the Lord.

"Here am I, the servant of the Lord; let it be with me according to your word" (Luke 1:38).

(ANNA CARTER FLORENCE)

Note

1. John Calvin, *Institutes of the Christian Religion,* III.xx.22 (Philadelphia: Westminster Press, 1960).

Prayers for Worship

CALLS TO WORSHIP

(Based on Psalm 89:1-4)

Leader: Sing, people of God, sing of God's steadfast love forever!

People: With our mouth we will proclaim the Lord's faithfulness to all generations.

Leader: Declare that steadfast love is forever established.

People: God's faithfulness is as firm as the heavens.

Leader: For a covenant has been made with the chosen one, and God has sworn it.

All: We will sing God's steadfast love forever!

(GAIL ANDERSON RICCIUTI)

(Based on Psalm 89)

Leader: I will sing of your steadfast love, O Lord, forever; with my mouth I will proclaim your faithfulness to all generations.

People: **I declare that your steadfast love is established forever; your faithfulness is as firm as the heavens.**

Leader: Let the heavens praise your wonders, O Lord, your faithfulness in the assembly of the holy ones. For who is as mighty as you, O Lord? Your faithfulness surrounds you. You rule the raging of the sea; when its waves rise, you still them.

People: **I declare that your steadfast love is established forever; your faithfulness is as firm as the heavens.**

Leader: Lord, where is your steadfast love of old, which by your faithfulness you swore to David? Remember, O Lord, how your servant is taunted; how I bear in my bosom the insults of the peoples, with which your enemies taunt, O Lord, with which they taunted the footsteps of your anointed.

People: **I declare that your steadfast love is established forever; your faithfulness is as firm as the heavens. Blessed be God forever.**

(SCOTT HALDEMAN)

Leader: Hear, O Israel: the Lord your God is one God!

People: **Hear, O Israel: God will make of you one everlasting house.**

Leader: Hear, O Israel: the Mighty One has done great things for us!

People: **Hear, O Israel: God has raised up the lowly, and filled the hungry with good things.**

All: **Let our souls magnify the Lord! Let us worship God!**

(ANNA CARTER FLORENCE)

PRAYER OF CONFESSION

(Based on Luke 1:45-55)

God of all promise, holy *is* your name. But we are forgetful of your mercy, consumed with personal struggles for status and survival. Forgive us, Mighty One, for disregarding you, the Source of our strength. Corral and quiet the proud strategies of our hearts, lest we be scattered far from your goodness. Fulfill our hungers with the nourishment of your spirit, lest in endless acquisition we find ourselves empty at last. We would offer our illusory powers into your hands, so that we might become your humble and thankful people once more, in Jesus' name.

(GAIL ANDERSON RICCIUTI)

ASSURANCE OF PARDON

Leader: In remembrance of his mercy, God has helped servant Israel. In Jesus Christ, we are forgiven.

People: **My soul magnifies the Lord!**

Leader: And blessed is the one who believes there will be a fulfillment of what the Lord has promised.

People: **My spirit rejoices in God my Savior!**

(GAIL ANDERSON RICCIUTI)

PRAYER OF CONFESSION

Eternal God, you have given us so much, and we have failed to be faithful. You give us mystery, and we deny its power. You give us prophecy, and we refuse its calling. You give us wisdom, and we behave foolishly. You shower us with blessings, and we sell them for the sake of our own vain desires. Forgive us, God. Help us do what is right, and say what is true, and love as passionately as you love. Give us the mind of Christ so that we might bring peace to this world. We pray in Jesus' name. Amen.

(ANNA CARTER FLORENCE)

ASSURANCE OF PARDON

Sisters and brothers, the good news is this: that while we make of this earth a poor thing, God in Christ is coming into the world to make straight all our paths, and to prepare the Lord's way. Hear the gospel this day: In Jesus Christ, you are forgiven. Thanks be to God.

(ANNA CARTER FLORENCE)

PASTORAL PRAYER

God of Saul and David, who raised up kings for your people, human rulers who brought peace and war, virtue and deceit, establish your reign of peace among us. Send to us One who will show us the way of mercy and love. God of Mary and Elizabeth, who gives children to the childless, who calls women to great acts of faith, reveal to us vocations of challenge and worth that we might participate in the revelation of your mysterious will. Bless all children and those who care for them. Strengthen all families, no matter the shape, of whatever size. Empower us for service that we may shelter those who are orphaned. Welcome those who are estranged. Feed those who are hungry. Mourn with those who grieve. Console those who despair. Visit those in prison. House those without shelter. God of our ancestors, who breaks our expectations and shatters our dreams, assuage our fears and come to us to make all things new. In the name of the One you sent and who will come again, to that One and to you

with the Holy Spirit, be all honor and glory, now and forever.
Amen.

(SCOTT HALDEMAN)

BENEDICTIONS

(Based on Romans 16:25-27)

Leader: May our wise and able God strengthen you,
through the precious mystery now revealed,
the prophetic message made known,
and the strong, compelling Spirit of faith.

People: **Glory to God forever, through Jesus Christ,
the revelation of Love! Amen.**

(GAIL ANDERSON RICCIUTI)

(Adapted from Romans 16:25-27)

Now may the gospel of Jesus Christ strengthen you,
The revelation of the mystery of the ages sustain you,
And the prophecy of God's holy word keep you in faith and
hope, both now and forevermore. Amen.

(ANNA CARTER FLORENCE)

ledge of salvation
ness of their sins, And they

READINGS

Isaiah 9:2-7

Psalm 96

Titus 2:11-14

Luke 2:1-14 (15-20)

A New Community

ISAIAH 9:2-7

The gifts we give at Christmas, and the ways in which we receive them, show a lot about who we are. Every family has its traditions, and it's important that the process of unwrapping be done in the proper way. Of course, what is "proper" varies from household to household.

For some of us, the unwrapping will begin right after church on Christmas Eve. For others, it will mean leaping out of bed as early as possible on Christmas Day or rolling out of bed as late as possible—children and adults tend to pull in different directions on that one. It may mean everybody taking turns to open and discuss and admire; it may mean everybody ripping into a stack of presents and showing them off afterward. It's not just what's in the package that matters; how we get to it is important as well.

And tonight is the time when the expectation is highest. The time of preparation is over. We've listed and shopped and ordered and wrapped. Now—at last—it's almost time to start unwrapping.

I'm not just humoring the children here—Christmas is not a celebration particular to children. Fellow grown-ups, let's not be too adult about it. Every one of us needs to receive presents as well as to give them. We need signs of love, tokens that someone else knows and cares who we are and what we enjoy. In particular, every one of us needs to receive the present we celebrate tonight.

Jesus, the child of God, came into the lives of Mary and Joseph as a gift—a firstborn son, the continuation of their heritage and their families. He came to the shepherds as a gift: "To you is born this day in the city of David a Savior." He comes to us as a gift as well. The most important Christmas present of all is not something that waits for you at home under the tree, but the gift God has given to all of us together. Jesus is our Christmas present.

He's harder to unwrap than the presents tied up in paper and ribbon. We won't get Jesus all unwrapped tonight, or tomorrow, or in the next twelve days. As he lived on the earth—the child of Mary and Joseph and Israel—the gift of God-with-us kept getting unwrapped, layer after layer. It was unwrapped as Jesus grew and taught and healed and lived and died and rose. We continue to unwrap it as the church struggles with times that change and human nature that stays the same.

In the gift of Jesus, the love of God (which is what we need the most) is given to us in different ways, according to our needs. When he was born at Bethlehem, Jesus was like a box that hadn't been opened yet. The ribbon and the wrapping were pulled away as he taught and helped people and made them well. People thought he was a troublemaker, and they killed him for it—which is even sadder than when your best present gets broken on Christmas morning. But this present didn't stay broken. Because God, who is at work in the world to fix what is broken, raised Jesus from the dead. The world is broken, and so are we.

But "unto us is born a Savior." That's our Christmas present.
Tonight, and tomorrow,
through the twelve days of Christmas,
and all the years of your life—
keep unwrapping![1]

(MARJORIE A. MENAUL)

Note

1. Adapted from *The Book of Occasional Services* (New York: The Church Hymnal Corporation, 1979), 21.

Keep Unwrapping

LUKE 2:1-14 (15-20)

Giving birth is a community event. Oh, don't get me wrong. I'm not one of those courageous souls who invites the extended family and NBC into the labor and delivery room. In fact, I threatened my husband with bodily harm if he so much as went for a camera during our children's births. There is a reason I believe that the sign to the shepherds was a baby already born and lying in a manger, and not a pregnant woman. Poor Mary didn't need all those shepherds and wise men hanging around for the birth.

But since I was a pastor in a small town, my pregnancies were community events. There was no hiding my morning sickness as I crawled into the pulpit on Sunday mornings armed with ginger ale and nausea wristbands. My baby showers were congregational events, well attended by men and women alike. Gruff, retired trustees who had never before attended a shower stood sheepishly against the walls, waiting with childlike expectation until I opened their gifts. Young fathers stood in silent camaraderie with my husband. And in my quiet moments of pondering, I was moved by their celebration, for at some level I sensed that unto *us* these children had been born.

But isn't the birth of any child a communal event? When we hear of a child born to a coworker or neighbor, don't we also rejoice? We put signs in the front yard so that total strangers will know, "It's a Girl!" We send cards and put announcements in the paper, because somehow we understand the miracle of a new birth is God's gift to us all.

Why should it surprise us, then, that the sign of God's redemptive act is often the birth of a child? For Abraham, the sign of God's coming was Isaac; for Hannah, the sign was Samuel. For Isaiah and the whole people of God who stood thirsting for God's redemption, the promise again is a child. And the name of this child is "Wonderful Counselor, Mighty God, Everlasting Father, Prince of Peace."

What hope Judah must have had for this child! A child who would one day lead the nation out of the darkness of its brokenness and sin into the dawn of a restored covenant with God. A child whose reign would embrace both justice and mercy and whose rule would strike that delicate balance between gentleness and strength. If the birth of an ordinary child draws the community together in shared joy and wonder, how much more would this special child break down the "we-they" divisions within Israel and restore Israel to an "us" again? What songs must have greeted this child's coming!

Is it any wonder, then, that Isaiah's song echoes through the songs of the angels on that miraculous night when Jesus is born? We've all read the scholars who wisely warn us against jumping too quickly from Isaiah to Jesus. Isaiah isn't even mentioned in Luke's telling of the story. But how can we help hearing the strains of Isaiah's song reverberating through the Christmas story? Wouldn't our hearts sing it even if the lectionary chose a different Old Testament text for Christmas Eve? More than any other birth, doesn't this birth give all creation reason to rejoice? More than any other child, isn't this child given to us all?

But what about that "us" in the story? Deep down, aren't we just a little tempted to believe that the miraculous story belongs more to Mary and the shepherds than it does to *us?* Have we heard the angels call *our* name, just as they called Mary's? Have we really heard that this child is good news for *us,* just as he was for the shepherds? Have we, like Joseph, been able to accept that the story is about *us* even if our names aren't in the head-lines?

"Us" is a key word in the Christmas story. "Us" makes the manger a personal invitation. "Us" means that our lives and this child's life are eternally intertwined. As long as this child belongs just to Mary and Joseph, we don't have to wonder why God lies before us in a trough filled with scratchy old hay, like a sack of feed for the animals.

The truth is we don't want to hear the "us" in Isaiah's song because we don't like having to admit that God had to go to such desperate measures to bring us back. We don't like to confess this Christmas that our lives are less than perfect, that deep down we're not quite as happy as we would like everyone to believe. There are wounds, cleverly hidden, festering in our hearts. There are secret pockets of bitterness, where the refresh-ing waters of forgiveness have simply dried up. There are the cobwebs of doubt, where we secretly wonder why the angels always sing for the house next door, but never for us. And if we admit to ourselves that we are the "us" to whom this child is given, we might also have to admit that we are the "us" for whom this Christ Child died. The reality of Isaiah's "us" is that this child in the manger didn't just come to us. He came for us.

In the movie *Field of Dreams,* a child of the 1960s turned Iowa farmer suddenly hears a voice telling him to plow up his fields and build a baseball field. "If you build it, he will come," says the voice. Ray obeys the voice and finishes the field. The voice visits again, telling Ray, "Ease his pain." Mystified by whose pain he is supposed to heal, Ray begins a long search for the one who will be healed by this cornfield turned baseball diamond. One day, Ray's father, who had died before Ray had ever had a chance to build any kind of meaningful relationship with him, appears on the field for a game with the other ballplayers. With tears in his eyes, Ray believes he has finally found the one in need of healing. "Ease his pain," murmurs Ray. As his father steps across the field for which Ray labored, Ray says "It was you."

"No, Ray," says one of the players, gently. "It was you." It was for you.

It was for you that Jesus came. It was for your hurts, your sins, your failings, your broken heart that he lay in the manger that night. It was for your doubt, your grief, your anger that he gave it all, nothing held back. It was because you were in the dark and he wanted to be the light that would guide you back home. It was because you were deaf and he wanted you to hear. It wasn't just for the shepherds or for Mary or for the Magi that he came. It was for you. It was for you.

The transforming moment of Christmas comes when we claim our place at the manger. When we realize that the Christ Child has come, not just for the world, but for us. When we realize that Jesus came because of our sin, that he walked to the cross breathing our name. It is not just world peace he promises, but our peace. It is not just the world's story that needs to be changed, but our story. It is for our transgressions that the Christ Child will one day be pierced; it is for our iniquities that he will be crushed.

But it is also the humble acceptance of this gift of manger and cross, grave and resurrection, that transforms the "we-they" attitude of our fractured world into a true "us." Around the manger, a new community is born. The excited shepherds share their story; a loving mother shares her son. The Magi give gifts; the innkeepers supply hay. Rich and poor, Gentile and Jew, migrant and landowner, male and female are transformed into the kind of "us" possible only with the love of this child, the one called Prince of Peace. My prayer this Christmas is that we will not only remember Isaiah's song but also sing it with the joy of knowing that it is our song as well. My prayer is that we will be among those who are so transformed by that child sleeping in the manger that we shall be the seeds of that new community, a place where there is no more "we-they," only "us." My prayer is that throughout this coming year, we will be among those who see the fulfillment of Isaiah's song and Isaiah's hope and claim the promise of Isaiah's God.

"For a child has been born for *us,* a son given to *us;* authority rests upon his shoulders; and he is named Wonderful Counselor, Mighty God, Everlasting Father, Prince of Peace" (Isa. 9:6, emphasis added).

(CATHERINE ERSKINE BOILEAU)

Prayers for Worship

CALLS TO WORSHIP

(Based on Isaiah 9 and Luke 2)

The people who walked in darkness have seen a great light; those who lived in a land of deep darkness—on them light has shined.

Glory to God in the highest heaven,
and on earth, peace among those whom God favors.

(MARJORIE A. MENAUL)

Leader: There's a song in the air. Will you sing it?

People: Let us sing to the Lord a new song.

Leader: There's a star in the sky. Will you follow it?

People: Let us abandon our darkness and embrace the light.

Leader: There's a mother's deep prayer. Will you breathe it?

People: Let us repent of our shallowness and ponder his coming.

Leader: And a baby's low cry. Will you adore him?

People: **Let us worship the Lord Jesus Christ.**[1]

(Catherine Erskine Boileau)

Note

1. Adapted from Josiah G. Holland, "There's a Song in the Air," 1874.

PRAYER OF CONFESSION

O God, our light, if ever there were a people who need your light, it is us. If ever there were a place where hope needed to be born, it is in the manger of our hearts. The work of your hands surrounds us, the miracle of your coming confronts us, but we remain weary of heart. We hear the songs of angels but cannot muster the joy to sing. You call us, like shepherds of old, to your manger to worship, but our minds wander.

O Jesus, who never tires of loving us, intervene in our history once more. Forgive our complacency. Come, be born in our hearts anew, that your light might blaze through our lives, that nations might gather at your manger, and that your name might be exalted in all the earth. Amen.

(Catherine Erskine Boileau)

ASSURANCE OF PARDON

The true home for Jesus on earth is not a manger but an open, repentant heart. Open your hearts, that you might find forgiveness for your sin and the salvation of your souls.

(Catherine Erskine Boileau)

PRAYER OF CONFESSION

Leader: God sent God's Son into the world to shine the
               light of his truth into our hearts and to set us free

— 136 —

from the darkness of despair. Let us confess our
sin and open ourselves to God's gracious forgiveness in Jesus Christ. Let us pray:

Eternal God, Mary rejoiced in your call to bear
the Christ Child. We do not always heed your call
to us as joyfully. We reject your claim on our lives,
following instead our selfish ways.

People: **Forgive us and remake us, O Lord.**

Leader: Jesus was born in humble circumstances and
wandered the land to preach and teach. We insist
on our own comforts while ignoring the poverty
and needs of others. We pursue material riches at
the expense of the impoverishment of our souls.

People: **Forgive and remake us, O Lord.**

Leader: Angels proclaimed the "good news of great joy"
that had come into the world with the birth of the
Christ Child. We are timid in sharing the good
news of your truth with our world.

People: **Forgive us and remake us, O Lord.**

Leader: The shepherds watching their flocks on the hill-
side near Bethlehem followed with wonder to see
the great thing God had done. We remain
entrenched in familiar, comfortable places, failing
to see the new things you are doing in our lives.

People: **Forgive us and remake us, O Lord, we pray.
Amen.**

(*Marjorie A. Menaul*)

BENEDICTIONS

Leader: Go forth in joy! For unto us a child is born, unto us a son is given.

People: And his name shall be called Wonderful Counselor, Mighty God, Everlasting Father, Prince of Peace.

(CATHERINE ERSKINE BOILEAU)

May Christ, who in the Incarnation gathered into one things earthly and heavenly, fill us and all creation with joy and peace. Amen.[1]

(MARJORIE A. MENAUL)

Note

1. Adapted from *The Book of Occasional Services* (New York: The Church Hymnal Corporation, 1979), 21.

READINGS

Isaiah 61:10–62:3

Psalm 148

Galatians 4:4-7

Luke 2:22-40

Can God's Future Justify Our Present?

ISAIAH 61:10–62:3

These are words of hope for beleaguered people of faith, especially those who may not be ready to hear or believe them. Hope is a funny thing. It is fragile, yet it can withstand anything. Hope does not always need a reason. Sometimes hope is its own reason. We who trust in God may wonder at times if God is paying attention and, if so, why is God not doing anything. When the promises of God seem to fail, scripture calls us to hope by making even grander promises. In the end we must either give ourselves up to despair or believe that God can create a future that justifies the present.

The Word of God Back Then

Isaiah 56–66 comes from a difficult time in Judah's history, the period of reconstruction following the exile. The prophets had warned of destruction and exile, but when it came to pass at the hands of the Babylonians, they changed their tune to promises of redemption and restoration. The vision they held before the people was inspiring. Read Isaiah 40–55 for one prophet's take on God's future work. The vision in a nutshell is that God is going to do some mighty work and set everything right.

Imagine the epidemic of optimism among the people when the Persian King Cyrus took control of their world and decreed they could return to their land and rebuild Jerusalem and its temple. The promises of God were coming true! Somehow, though, the reality never quite lived up to the vision. The temple would not be reconstructed until 515 B.C.—23 years after Cyrus's decree. The people had lived on the dreams spun by the prophets, but now they were struggling, and God seemed to be far away. Nothing was right, and they were losing hope.

The word of the Lord came to those people in the form of our text. Again, amazing promises were made, promises contradicted by reality as they saw it. With the promises, however, came hope and the glorious possibility that God might set things right after all.

The Word of God Now

I want to ask you to believe something so wonderful you will not be able to imagine it. I want you to believe that God can create a future that justifies the present. God can bring about a state of affairs that will justify all the evil and suffering from the beginning of creation until the consummation of God's saving work. When God's saving work is finished, we will look around, reflect on all that has come before, and say, "Now I see. It was a good plan. God was bringing us to this, and it was worth all the pain and sorrow." I know how crazy that sounds, and how difficult such faith is. Personally, I admit to not being able to begin to imagine how God might do that. When I think of the suffering of a child or the larger-than-life evil of the holocaust, I do not think it possible.

However, although it seems impossible, I must believe it. Why? First, because reality has never approximated the marvelous promises made through the prophets. I believe those promises are good. They came closer to fulfillment in Jesus' life, death, and resurrection. And they will prove true when God's kingdom comes in its fullness. Second, because of the resurrection. By raising Jesus from the dead, God showed the love and power necessary to bring good out of evil and victory from defeat. Just as the resurrection vindicated the cross, so God's consummation will vindicate history. Although it may be unimaginable, you must believe it. God has more imagination than we do, so we must not give up hope. Amen.

(DAVID C. MAULDIN)

To Be Inside Where We Belong

GALATIANS 4:4-7

Paul wrote to the Galatians with a lot on the line. All his work among them was in the balance. False teachers had come to the church, adding to the gospel Paul had preached to them. Paul had taught that a person is put right with God through faith in Jesus Christ. His opponents said faith is not enough because the true Christian is one who keeps the Law of Moses. They advocated Jewish food laws, circumcision (for the men), and careful attention to the Jewish calendar of holy days. The epistle reading is a beautiful part of the fiery letter Paul wrote to defend his teaching.

On the Outside Looking In

Have you ever been on the outside looking in? Perhaps you were the one kid left off the invitation list. Or maybe you were kept out of the loop at the office when important information was secretly circulating. Most of us have felt excluded at some point, and we know that standing on the outside is not a good feeling. In a way, the issue in Galatia and our passage are about who is inside and who is outside.

Paul's opponents were surely not malicious people. They were corrupting the gospel and destroying the church, but that was not their intention. From their perspective, anyone who did not follow the Law of Moses was on the outside, the outside of God's good graces. The Law, with its dietary restrictions and festivals, had always been the special possession of God's inner circle. They thought Paul was wrong when he said faith, apart from the Law, opened the door.

Paul saw the Law differently. He knew faith put one on the inside. The Law had its place, but it kept people on the outside. Paul argued that, before Jesus, not only were Gentiles on the outside (his opponents would have agreed with that) but Jews too were outside. In Romans 11:32, Paul wrote, "God has imprisoned all in disobedience so that he may be merciful to all." The same idea appears in Galatians, again in vivid metaphor. "Before faith came, we were imprisoned and guarded under the Law" (Gal. 3:23). The Law did not place one on the inside. Jew and Gentile alike needed faith, and faith alone.

Just before our passage, Paul compares the Jews, who had the Law, to heirs who had been minors. They had been promised a place on the inside, but they had not taken their rightful place yet. They were still outside, like the Gentiles. But, in the fullness of time, God provided a way for Jew and Gentile alike to move from the outside to the inside.

Adoption

How many creative ways we find here to describe what happens when God moves us from the outside to the inside! God does not just bring us in; God adopts us. We are no longer slaves (outside). We are heirs (inside). I hope all of you know the joy and happiness that come from the feeling that you truly belong.

You should, because God has done something wonderful for you through Jesus Christ. You are allowed on the inside. More than that, you are adopted. You truly belong.

How do we know this? God has sent the Holy Spirit into our hearts. The Spirit cries, "Abba! Father!" *Abba* is the Aramaic word for "father," and we find it on the lips of Jesus in the Gospel of Mark. Jesus taught his followers to refer to God with this word, and Paul reads significance into it. If we may properly address God as "Father," then God has adopted us. If God has adopted us, then we belong; we are on the inside—not as visitors or foreigners but as children and heirs.

(DAVID C. MAULDIN)

Breaking Forth in Wonder

LUKE 2:22-40

What a woman we meet in this Anna, introduced to us at the presentation of the baby Jesus in the temple! She had much against her: she was a woman, a widow, and old. In society's eyes, she was of little importance. The cultural values of her time associated men with honor, and women with shame. In like manner, age was associated with weakness, female widowhood with need. While men were easily recognized as spiritual leaders, women's spirituality was more often than not viewed as contingent upon and even secondary to men's.

The Gospel story for this first Sunday after Christmas, however, continues the surprising revelation of the fullness God's grace manifested by Jesus' birth. In the birth of the Christ Child, a new era begins, and all creation is called to break forth in wonder. For the light of grace revealed in this child, Jesus, casts an aura upon all who encounter him. It is a light that radiates from the tiny person at the center of the scene described in the Gospel reading. It is a light that reflects upon old Simeon and causes all of us to see a new dimension, a new era. That new era also shines forth gloriously in old Anna's behavior.

In Anna's speech-act the old oppressive patterns of gender, age, and marital status begin to crumble. She has encountered the liberating God in Jesus. Through the lens of spiritual discernment she sees the promised salvation, a salvation that brings to flower the words of the ancient psalm for this day: "Young men and women alike, old and young together! Let them praise the name of the LORD" (Ps. 148:12-13a). And decades after the presentation of Jesus in the temple, the apostle Paul can say confidently that Anna and all other people to whom society pays little or no honor—children, women, slaves, the elderly, the differently abled—all are in Jesus Christ equal before God. In fact, Paul claims that Anna is an heir with Christ of the fullness of God's riches. Such a gift of grace is enough to cause Anna—and all of us—to break forth in wonder before the incarnate God, Emmanuel.

In the moving tableau in the temple, more attention is given to Simeon, who is said to have been guided by the Spirit. It is Simeon who takes the child in his arms and blesses Mary and Joseph. It is Simeon who in compassion warns Mary of the pain she will endure. It is Simeon who gives the church what has come to be a beloved canticle, "Now let your servant depart in peace"—a phrase that was also used at times when slaves were freed. (The first words of the phrase are familiar in the Latin title of the canticle, "Nunc Dimittis.")

But there are parallels between Simeon and Anna, and they are remarkable. Both Simeon and Anna are old. Both are pious, righteous, and devout. Both are looking for the coming of the one who was to become salvation for Israel. Both had their spiritual eyes open to recognize in this child the promised one. However, while Simeon, after praising God for the gift, spoke only to Joseph and Mary, Anna went out and spoke to "*all* who were looking for the redemption of Jerusalem" (Luke 2:38, emphasis added).

She, who like other women was confined to the outer courts

of the temple because of her gender, here joins Simeon and breaks forth in wonder. But she goes further! In Luke's Gospel, Anna becomes the first human evangelist, one who tells others the good news—others not present at the temple, other outsiders, others hoping for salvation. With the prophet Isaiah of old, Anna is moved from the wonder of the luminous scene at the temple to exclaim, "For Zion's sake I will not keep silent" (Isa. 62:1*a*). She has encountered in the child the wonder of the grace of God, the liberating, life-giving, barrier-breaking wonder of God in Christ, before whom there are no gender, age, race, or status walls. She has a voice, and her breaking forth in wonder is heard beyond the temple's walls, heard by those who had long sat in the darkness of night. Her evangel song is Simeon's song: "These eyes have seen salvation's dawn. . . . This is the savior of the world, the Gentiles' promised light, God's glory dwelling in our midst, the joy of Israel."[1]

Thus Simeon and Anna both proclaim the new reality of the one who will bring salvation for all people. The ones whom society diminishes God exalts. The ones who were once outsiders become the very ones about whom it is said, "You shall be a crown of beauty in the hand of the LORD, and a royal diadem in the hand of your God" (Isa. 62:3).

That is the gospel news this first Sunday after Christmas: In Jesus Christ no one is slave to sin, separated from God by distinctions or limitations of any form. Rather each one is a child of God and heir with Christ through the grace of God (Gal. 4:7).

The church has prized this story and the message it conveys so much that it has used Simeon's peaceful canticle at a critical juncture in its own liturgical life. At the conclusion of the celebration of the Eucharist, the church has traditionally sung, "Now let your servant depart in peace." For the church has recognized that in the breaking of bread, we, like Simeon and Anna, encounter God in Jesus Christ, and hope and grace are born anew. At the table, the church meets the one before whom, in the words of John Calvin, all we can do is "break forth in wonder."[2]

But the church has done more than contemplate the beauty of

God's incarnate grace in the sanctuary or at the table. Throughout history the church has also been compelled to go out, like Anna, taking with it in life and speech the gospel of grace. Like Anna, we are compelled to shine upon the world the fullness of the gospel news of redemption. Following the steps of the old, widowed woman Anna, who out of oppression's grip was silent no longer, we go out to become instruments of redemption, righteousness, and peace. Anna lived out Simeon's song. A freed slave who departed from the holy place in peace, Anna went out in joy, a new woman, a new being, empowered for life, eager to share the grace that she had found.

The invitation this first Sunday after Christmas is the same one proclaimed from Anna's heart long ago. For the child whom Simeon and Anna first extolled is the same child who later gave his life so that salvation could come to all who sit in darkness— so that *all* with Simeon and Anna might break forth in wonder and sing, "These eyes have seen salvation's dawn."

(GLÁUCIA VASCONCELOS WILKEY)

Notes

1. From the paraphrase of the words of Simeon in James Quinn, "Song of Simeon," in *The Presbyterian Hymnal* (Louisville: Westminster John Knox Press, 1990), 603.

2. John Calvin, *Institutes of Christian Religion*, ed. John McNeill, trans. Ford L. Battles (Philadelphia: Westminster, 1960), 4.17.4, p. 1367.

Prayers for Worship

CALL TO WORSHIP

A Litany

[Note: All responses are to be sung in the key of G major, using tunes from the following carols: "Angels We Have Heard on

High" (Refrain, first line); "O Little Town of Bethlehem" (fourth stanza, second line); and "See Amid the Winter's Snow" (Refrain).]

Creator God,
Earth and sky join the song
the angels sing:
Gloria in Excelsis Deo

Jesus Christ,
You dwelt among us
and we found grace.

Gloria in Excelsis Deo

Holy Spirit,
Your gentle voice assures us
that in Christ we inherit God's riches.

Gloria in Excelsis Deo

Holy Triune God,
when our sins keep us as slaves,

Cast out our sin and enter in,
Be born in us today

When we fail to see you
in the guise of the oppressed,

Cast out our sin and enter in,
Be born in us today

When we are satisfied with
sanctuary rituals
and fail to take salvation's dawn
to the darkness of the world,

Cast out our sin and enter in,
be born in us today

Grace-giving God,
in your coming all women find strength,
all men find gentleness,
all youth find wisdom,
all aged find joy.

As Simeon and Anna of old
recognized and sang your glory,
so lead us to see salvation's dawn,
and break forth in wonder
in witness to the world.

Hail that ever blessed morn, Hail redemption's happy dawn,
Sing through all Jerusalem: Christ is born in Bethlehem.[1]

(GLÁUCIA VASCONCELOS WILKEY)

Note

1. Edward Caswell, "See Amid the Winter's Snow," in *The Presbyterian Hymnal* (Louisville: Westminster/John Knox, 1990), 51.

READINGS

Isaiah 60:1-6

Psalm 72:1-7, 10-14

Ephesians 3:1-12

Matthew 2:1-12

Come Toward the Light

ISAIAH 60:1-6

The first strophe of this salvation poem summarizes the rest of the poem. Take note of the repetition of the word *come* throughout the passage. The central word is "glory" (*kabhod*). In verse 1, "Arise, shine" is an invitation to Israel to bask in God's glory. Israel had known darkness. Now God's glory "shines" and Israel is invited to respond to this manifestation by rising from its despair. The light itself is a gift of God, a chance for Jerusalem to glow for all to see. The light is also God *come* and Israel's only source of hope. Verse 2 expresses the contrast between "light" and "darkness," the difference between Jerusalem filled with God's glory, and the rest of the world. Verse 3 tells how all nations will *come* to the light. It may be summarized by Isaiah 40:5: "The glory of the LORD shall be revealed, and all people shall see it together."

I. Come to the Light

In the second stanza, the poet uses words to create a picture of what is taking place if Israel will only look. Others will see Jerusalem reflecting the glory and will come. They are drawn by the light. Sons and daughters of Israel will return, those who have been scattered away from home long after the official homecoming. They will return with wealth from other nations and bring it to the altar (v. 7). When Israel sees, emotions will change from despair to joy, like a mother who has not seen her children in years. There is a thrill that comes with the glorious return.

II. Come to Worship

Verse 6 tells of others who are coming and bringing exotic gifts such as gold and frankincense. This shows that the nations too are coming to submit themselves to God's new future. All go before the altar to behold God's glory. God's presence gives the gift of life to Jerusalem and all the nations.

I write this during my son Andrew's first Christmas. We brought Andrew into the living room to see the Christmas tree for the first time, and he was amazed as we plugged in the lights for the tree. Ever since, he has been drawn by the light to come and investigate the tree. In the eyes of this young child, I see the wonder, curiosity, and joy that the light on the tree brings him.

We all sometimes need to be reminded that we are God's children who need to come to the "light" as well. Just as Jerusalem was to be the light on a hill for all nations to see God's glory, we need to come toward this "light" so that we too may be transformed by life in God's presence. This life in the presence of God should be one of wonder, curiosity, and joy, like that of a young child. By acknowledging and being transformed by the "light," we too can participate in God's kingdom. The essence of the passage is reflected in the hymn "Arise, Your Light Is Come" by Ruth Duck: "Show forth the glory of your God / Which shines on you today."[1]

(MARCIA T. THOMPSON)

Note

1. Ruth Duck, "Arise, Your Light Is Come," in *Dancing in the Universe: Hymns and Songs* (Chicago: G.I.A., 1992), #39.

Share the Secret

EPHESIANS 3:1-12

The Ron Mason family enjoyed the best this life had to offer. Ron had done well. There was nothing they wanted that they didn't get.

The Don Mason family lacked all but the essentials. Don had been ill most of his adult life, and his only attempt at running a business had failed.

Although they were brothers, Ron and Don, along with their families, lived in different worlds. The Ron Mason cousins had always felt, talked, and acted superior to their Don Mason cousins. They wore their privileged status conspicuously, until the attorney's letter arrived from London with unexpected news.

Neither family had known of their very distant and wealthy English relative. This unknown uncle had recently died, leaving so large an inheritance that both the Ron Mason and the Don Mason families became equally wealthy.

The Don Masons celebrated the good news that had been secret all these years. The Ron Masons resented the secret news that practically eliminated them from their former superior position.

I. The Secret Is Out: The Gentiles Have Equal Standing Before God (vv. 1-6)

Not everybody wants a secret to be told. It was because Paul was telling the secret, God's divine mystery, that he had been imprisoned in Rome (v. 1). The faithful apostle had fulfilled his divine commission to share the secret (vv. 2-5). Paul called his message a "mystery." However, because he had shared this particular secret, the "establishment" was not happy.

What was the secret? That the Gentiles were

- equal heirs of the riches of God;
- equal members of the Body of Christ;
- equal sharers of the promises of God;
- right up there alongside the people of Israel (v. 6).

That was the problem. The apostles were the first to know of God's plan to make salvation universally available. And Paul couldn't keep this secret. When God broke the news that Gentiles could share equally in God's rich blessings, some Jewish elitists were not pleased. They didn't like the news, and they didn't like anybody who spread it. It made everybody too equal, too blessed. They had lost their superior position. That's why Paul was in jail. He had dared to "read the will" of God to the world.

II. Go Tell the Secret: God's Riches Are Available to All People (vv. 7-12)

Although Paul was nobody special (v. 8), he was made a steward of the news that the blessings of God have been made available to all people (vv. 7-10). According to the owner's will, the steward parcels out the owner's wealth and resources to those the owner directs. The great apostle was merely the "reader of the will," the steward of the good news that God's blessings are for all people.

This had always been God's ultimate plan. Salvation was not going to be limited to the Jews. Access to God was for all people who come to God through faith in Christ Jesus (vv. 11-12).

The privilege and responsibility of stewarding the secret mystery of God's universal offer of blessings have been passed down to all who inherit these blessings by faith in Christ. Those who know the secret pass it on to others, not only to their own but to all people everywhere.

I would enjoy being the reader and the steward of the will to the Mason families. I would love to see the look on the faces of the Don Masons when they realize they now possess every possible material and financial resource. I would also love to see the look on the faces of the Ron Masons when it dawns on them that their cousins are now their equals. What a shock. What a surprise. What a secret.

(TIMOTHY WARREN)

Christ's Love Is Like . . .

MATTHEW 2:1-12

This Gospel scripture invites us to reflect upon Christmas pageants, not just the first pageant—described in Matthew and Luke, where Magi, shepherds, and angels flow in and out of the stable in a loosely structured dance—but the many Christmas pageants that have been staged since. These seasonal pageants invite all of us to playfully engage in the wonder of God-made-flesh.

Do you remember what it was like to be an angel, or a shepherd, or a star for one hour? Remember trying on the costume while your heart tried on an angel's identity, a star's mystery, a shepherd's adventure? All over the globe, for hundreds of years, adults and children have reenacted the incarnation with a Christmas pageant. Whimsy and playfulness are meant to be important parts of Christmas!

We have a splendid pageant on Christmas Eve when some of our children wave a cosmos of stars into the empty space behind our main altar and others take on the role of halo-wearing angels or turban-wearing shepherds, all circling around the virgin and child who are seated at the base of the main altar. Usually a shepherd or two trip on their long tunics, the stars compete to see whose star is the tallest, and at least one angel cries, but the pageant is all the more wonderful because of that. No one acts stiff or artificial; real, little human beings are doing their best to welcome God. But like those of us who are observers, they carry their humanness with them.

Most serious scholars point out that the Gospels' birth narratives have not been substantiated by nonbiblical historical texts. Unlike other portions of the Old and New Testaments, there is no corroboration of any of the details Matthew presents to us in texts of Greek, Roman, Persian, or Aramaic origin. Neither do the birth narratives parallel any first-century Christian writing. So we scientific twentieth-century Christians cannot confirm that these detailed stories of shepherds or Magi actually happened as historical fact.

Yet one look at a Christmas pageant will tell us that the value of these stories is not based upon their factual reality—whatever that may be—but upon the spiritual truths they communicate. Like poetry or music or dance, these stories herald to the world the mystery and wonder of Christ's incarnation. Christ's birth resonates with so much significance that the cosmos itself could not remain neutral, so it produced a star. Christ's birth was so significant that wise astrologers from faraway places journeyed hundreds of miles because they read in heaven's alignment what most of Bethlehem couldn't read in Mary's face. Christ's birth was so significant that ever since those first wise men, men and women have been moved to great lengths to seek God and to celebrate when they found God.

The adoration of the Magi may be the first Bible story most of us learn. I knew it before I went to kindergarten because the basic plot is a simple one: dress up, get a make-believe gift, and hand it over to the baby. My strongest memory of a Christmas pageant comes from the Christmas when I was four. It was a pageant with only three characters, which took place in my parents' living room on a cold December afternoon.

My twin sister, Mary, and I were playing in the living room

while my oldest sister, Louise, listened to Beatles records upstairs and my mother cooked in the kitchen. When the doorbell rang and David, a college friend of my sister's, arrived, Mom asked him to wait in the living room while she went to retrieve Louise. To four-year-olds, any adult seemed to be fair game for playing, so Mary and I quickly pressed the unsuspecting guest into service, insisting that he take on the role of Mary, so that we could parade in with our gifts, as the wise men. To his credit, David grumbled only a little when we gave him a blue cocktail dress that had belonged to my grandmother; we insisted he wear it on his head, as a veil. Then the naked plastic baby doll was handed over and David knelt in front of the Christmas tree. Mary and I left the room to make an entrance just as my mother and older sister came down the stairs, so they got back to the living room before we did. What my oldest sister made of her date dressed up like the Virgin Mary, I do not know, but even though I was only four, I think I remember a gasp.

I do know I remember the thick silence in that room immediately preceding our enthusiastic performance. In we went, in my dad's shoes and coats, and we presented our gifts—a stone pillbox and a glass ashtray—to Mary and the baby. Over a decade later, I learned that David was from a conservative Jewish family and had vehement feelings about the Christian calendar's domination of American culture. He'd walked into our house that day and been turned into the overdressed focal point of a faith he didn't believe in and a culture he rejected; but he graciously entered our story anyway.

It has struck me since then that there is something appropriate in a Christmas pageant containing a conservative Jew's generosity to two little Gentile girls. Christ's becoming flesh and dwelling among us is at least as preposterous as a Jewish college man dressing up as the Virgin Mary. Christ's willingness to enter into the vulnerabilities and absurdities of humankind is well paralleled by David's respectful hold on our plastic baby Jesus. What is Christ's love for us like? Christ's love is like the bent body of a Jewish man wearing an old cocktail dress on his head, cradling a naked plastic baby doll. With all its silliness and social tension, that living room pageant points to a core truth about incarnation. God will enter into all the games we play and seek us while we play them. And God does not enter our games half-heartedly. "For God so loved the world that [God] gave [God's] only son, so that everyone who believes in him may not perish but may have eternal life" (John 3:16).

If many of us now feel too old for the physical playfulness of Christmas pageants, we will still be well served to play them in our imaginations. This year, as in every year, we are invited to decide where we stand in relation to the Christ. Where do you see yourself located in this year's manger scene? Each vantage point has its advantages and drawbacks. Are you drawn to the shepherds abiding in their fields, full of appreciation for open skies, busy with daily tasks, and still ready to make room to seek God? Or are you drawn to the vigor and restlessness of wise men, or the pondering, quiet wisdom of Mary? Perhaps you are a dove, hovering in the rafters, drowsy and comfortable, resting in Christ's presence, or perhaps you are a manger goat this year, vaguely aware that you are in the general vicinity of God but distracted by the cud you are chewing. If we're lucky, in our life span we will all play many roles. When you recognize your place in this year's manger scene, I invite you to tell at least one person so that you will have a comrade in the playful wisdom most of us took for granted as children.

Of course, if you take me up on my invitation, you will be taking a risk. Some adults might find your story to be so vulnerable that they won't know what to say. Then again, in response to your story, someone might tell you where *they* stand in relation to Christ this Christmas. There's no predicting what grace might provide in such a sacred game. Great wisdom and great peace can come out of tender moments. What is certain is that if we do tell our own story this Christmas, we will also be telling the story of stories afresh. We will be proclaiming that Christ is born and dwells with us. And when his story is set in motion, grace arrives to teach us, and love arrives to heal us. There's no telling what we might discover about God or ourselves in those stories.

When I reflect upon my relationship with Christ this December, I'm making the same choice I made when I was four; the vigor and adventure of the wise men energize me. I need to do some determined searching for God this year. But when I anticipate next year, I already have my eye on Mary and the dreaming wisdom that lets her rest in Christ's presence. For each of us, in this Epiphany there is a star to discover, a journey to take, a manger to rest within.

(MARGARET K. SCHWARZER)

Prayers for Worship

CALLS TO WORSHIP

(Adapted from Isaiah 60:1-7)

Leader: "Arise, shine; for your light has come."
            Lift up your eyes for the grace of God is near us.

**People: Holy One, we open our eyes;
            We lift our voices to you.**

Leader: "Arise, shine; for your light has come."
            Open your hearts, for the Prince of Peace is near
            us.

**People: Holy One, we open our hearts;
            We lift our voices to you.**

Leader: "Arise, shine; for your light has come."
            Rejoice; the righteousness and mercy of God dwell
            with us.

People: **Holy One, we rejoice;**
We lift our voices to you.

(MARGARET K. SCHWARZER)

(Based on Psalm 72)

Leader: O God, judge your people with righteousness, and your poor with justice.

People: **May the mountains yield prosperity for the people, and the hills blossom in righteousness.**

Leader: May your governor defend the cause of the poor of the people, give deliverance to the needy, and crush the oppressor.

People: **May he live while the sun endures, and as long as the moon, throughout all generations.**

Leader: In the days of your servant, may righteousness flourish and peace abound.

People: **Blessed be the Lord, the God of Israel, who alone does wondrous things.**

(SCOTT HALDEMAN)

(Based on Psalm 72:1-7)

Leader: Give the king your justice, O God,

People: **and your righteousness to the royal son!**

Leader: May he judge your people with righteousness,

People: **and your poor with justice!**

Leader: Let the mountains bear prosperity for the people, and the hills, in righteousness!

People: May he defend the cause of the poor of the people, give deliverance to the needy, and crush the oppressor!

Leader: May he live while the sun endures, and as long as the moon, throughout all generations!

People: May he be like rain that falls on the mown grass, like showers that water the earth!

Leader: In his days may righteousness flourish, and peace abound, till the moon be no more!

(THOMAS GILDERMEISTER)

PRAYER OF CONFESSION

Gracious God, we are a sinful people. Often our hearts are cold and our faith is thin. In the midst of our broken world, our souls shrivel, and our bitterness expands. Refresh our hearts and renew our hopes. Kindle in us the delight and joy you gave us at our birth.

(MARGARET K. SCHWARZER)

ASSURANCE OF PARDON

Hear the good news. We are forgiven and called to new life through Jesus Christ our Lord. Our sins are forgiven in the name of God: maker of love, giver of life, redeemer of all. Amen.

(MARGARET K. SCHWARZER)

PASTORAL PRAYER

Savior of all peoples, who took on our flesh in a stable and slept in a box made for animal feed; sages followed a star to find you, paid you homage, and went home by another way. Be present among us. Encounter us in word, in bread, in song, in prayer. Touch us. Change us. Send us out to walk in new paths, telling your story, proclaiming good news to the nations. Light of the World, shine upon us. Shine your light of hope in the corners of gloom in our lives and throughout the streets of our cities and towns. Shine upon those who are lost to show them a new path home. Shine upon those who are ill to give them strength to decide how they shall live whole lives. Shine upon those in despair who need to make a way out of no way. Shine upon those whose homes, families, and bodies that war has torn apart; reveal a path to peace. Shine upon your creation, the earth and its creatures, things seen and unseen. Burn away the mist and let us see you face-to-face so that you can wipe away our tears and make death to be no more. Light of the World, we praise your name. Amen.

(SCOTT HALDEMAN)

BENEDICTION

May God's light inspire you;
May God's angels guide you;
May God's love protect you.
May Christ, our Emmanuel,
Dwell with you this day and forevermore. Amen.

(MARGARET K. SCHWARZER)

Year

C

READINGS

Jeremiah 33:14-16

Psalm 25:1-10

1 Thessalonians 3:9-13

Luke 21:25-36

Pre-Christmas Sale Hope

JEREMIAH 33:14-16

The season of Advent is a season of hope. Something is dawning on the horizon of our lives—can we see it? The very meaning of the season is about something or someone coming. The word *advent* is derived from the Latin word *adventus,* which literally means *coming.*

In this Advent season, the church lifts its collective head and squints toward the horizon. We take a long view, turning our gaze toward that which is approaching. On this first Sunday of Advent, our view may be a little cloudy. The horizon is faraway, and although we can see that something is happening, we cannot quite make out what it is.

To discern what is approaching, we listen to the words of the prophet Jeremiah. His words excite us because he promises salvation: "In those days and at that time I will cause a righteous Branch to spring up for David; and he shall execute justice and righteousness in the land" (v. 15). The name of this approaching one is "righteousness."

Thus, in Advent, the church proclaims the approaching righteousness of God. It is a crucial proclamation because it is a real source of hope. The world, our lives, our days cannot live without hope. Anticipating what God is going to do energizes us for faithful and fruitful living.

Ironically, we anticipate the future by remembering the past. We remember the glory days of Israel under King David's leadership. We strain forward in order to see "a righteous Branch" spring forth. But this is a particular kind of remembering. In this season we do not remember that which has happened in the past in a historic sense. We remember in a way that changes us. It is the memory of a lover's kiss, the memory of a child returning home after too long an absence, the memory of the words of forgiveness for some wrong committed. The power of this kind of memory can make us cry or laugh or even feel contentment. It is memory that never grows old. We tell the stories of it again and again because each time we tell the story we experience the power of the memory in our lives.

Each year the season of Advent calls the community of faith to prepare for the visit of God's salvation. Our work is to anticipate that which God will do to bring fulfillment to all people. We are preparing for the event in the stable at Bethlehem which brings together "the hopes and fears of all the years," as Phillips Brooks's "O Little Town of Bethlehem" so beautifully puts it.

Hope is never cheap. It demands the great energy of faith. This is true because we need hope when we face desperate circumstances. Jeremiah draws on the deep energy of his own faith as he proclaims that "the days are coming" (v. 14a NKJV). It must have been a difficult ministry because he was speaking to people who had lost hope. Exiles in a strange land do not find hope easily. Into this condition of lostness, the prophet dares to speak his word of hopeful newness that will come to pass because of God's salvation. Like Jeremiah, the church must draw on its energy of faith as it offers to the world a vision of the newness that God brings in the birth of Christ. The proclamation must be bold so that our anticipation can be without hesitation. "The days are coming," and we must make ready. So, lift your heads and let your hearts be strengthened. God is doing a new thing, and to us has come the joyous and holy task of helping the world get ready for the most blessed event of history!

(CHRIS ANDREWS)

Encouraging One Another

1 THESSALONIANS 3:9-13

As children growing up, we all remember the old saying: "Sticks and stones may break my bones, but words will never hurt me." Although this defensive response may sound good, the reality is that words do have the power to hurt—or to heal. Timothy has returned to Paul in Corinth with a report from the church in Thessalonica. It is a good report. Despite some theological disputes regarding the *parousia,* the church is thriving in the face of persecution from the Jews. Paul is pleased with their progress, and the pericope for this first Sunday of Advent is a word of great encouragement for the spiritual growth of those who are faithful.

In the context of the Advent season's theme of waiting and watching, what better word for us than the need for us to encourage one another in our spiritual growth? In a setting of persecution, Paul seeks to gently nurture this new congregation as it seeks to grow in reaching out to others. Paul shares his joy at their growth and work. Paul also pledges to come soon to see them and to celebrate and continue to nourish them in their faith. These are good words for us even now. We live in a culture that is quick to judge and one in which the tabloids are ready and waiting to divulge and exploit the latest gossip. On television we can now watch a game show host ridicule people for pure entertainment value. We know how easy it is to feel isolated and unworthy in such a culture. Advent is about seeking to proclaim that all is not lost. We do have a hope that is eternal and true. However, such hoping is not done watching the clock. Rather, such a hoping demands a response of actively living out in life what we know to be true in our heart.

Paul's perspective is one of praise and nurture for those who need to know that they are a part of God's work in the world. Paul believed that God was at work in history. Paul's letters are full of his sense of that work and the need for people to join in that work. As Paul hears the good news from Thessalonica, his response is one of praise and one of promise that they will continue. Paul is excited about the new converts to the faith and their faithful response in the wake of persecution and hatred. The waiting of Advent is not about sitting on a fence post daydreaming of what may happen next. The waiting of Advent is about growing in the love of God, sharing that love with others, and partnering with God in proclaiming the meaning that love brings. Etty Hillesum, a Dutch Jew, voluntarily went to and died in a Nazi concentration camp because she felt that "a camp needs a poet, one who experiences life there, even there, as a bard and is able to sing about it."[1] The following is a diary entry as she watches the Nazi net tighten around the Jews.

> Monday morning, 10 o'clock. . . . The latest news is that all Jews will be transported out of Holland through Drenthe Province and then on to Poland. . . . And yet I don't think life is meaningless. And God is not accountable to us for the senseless harm we cause one another. We are accountable to Him! . . . And yet I find life beautiful and meaningful. From minute to minute. . . . Sun on the balcony and a light breeze through the jasmine. . . . I shall linger another ten minutes with the jasmine, and then to see the friend . . . who can still suddenly present me with an aspect so new that I catch my breath with surprise. How exotic the jasmine looks, so delicate and dazzling against the mud-brown walls. I can't take in how beautiful this jasmine is. But there is no need to. It is enough

simply to believe in miracles in the twentieth century. And I do, even though the lice will be eating me up in Poland before long.[2]

Paul celebrates and seeks to nurture such a perspective as he hears the good news from Timothy about the power of God being lived out through a church in Thessalonica. Regardless of how things may appear, the word of God proclaims a word of hope, encouragement, praise, and joy. Our world is waiting desperately to hear such words.

(*TRAVIS FRANKLIN*)

Notes

1. Arnos Pomerans, trans., *An Interrupted Life: The Diaries of Etty Hillesum 1941–1943* (New York: Pantheon Books, 1983), 190.
2. Ibid., 127-28.

Watch, Wait, and Wonder

LUKE 21:25-36

This is the beginning of a new age. We have weathered apocalyptic predictions of signs of the end time. After twenty centuries, wars, poverty, and injustice still reign. The world is racked with violence, yet not destroyed. It is filled with destruction, yet not overcome. We live amidst injustice, poverty, and prejudice, yet still there are signs of justice, fullness, and hope. And we watch. And we wait. And we wonder.

Recently I was driving a long and boring (that is, not full of distractions) section of Interstate 20 between South Carolina and Georgia. It is a stretch of road that symbolizes movement from the past to the present. It denotes movement from one home to another, one season to the next, one world to another. It literally is the road from my former life to my present life. I found myself carefully watching the rearview mirror as I drove, looking back on where I had been.

The year had been monumentally eventful. My only child, my woman child, had graduated from college. My mother, having lived every day of her eighty-three and a half years, had died on the second Sunday of Advent. She was now free from years of living with sickeningly chronic blood diseases, probably contracted from her life's work as a nurse anesthetist. A year had passed since my child's graduation and six months since my mother's untimely, timely death.

Grief was taking hold of my body. I was tired. Some nights were sleepless. Restlessness marked many days. An ordinary experience could touch deep sadness. The past few weeks had marked several anniversaries: Mother's Day, leaving me motherless; her May birthday; the anniversary of my sister's tragic death some twenty-five years ago. My rich life as a pastor to a university community was all too often filled with experiences of death and grief. Absence created sorrow which was difficult to bear. There was little in which I found great comfort. Friends, food, busyness, sleep, gardening—all stirred memories which, in this season, felt like too much absence and emptiness.

Looking into the rearview mirror called me to the former things, the former days. Life as a child. Life as a mother. Life in ministry. Life in a full and yet finally failed marriage. Looking back stirred reminders of tragedy, death, sorrow. And looking back stirred reminders of love, life, parties, celebrations, joys, and creativity. Looking back conjured up memories which served as reminders of what would never again be and grief which was being transformed into something new and different.

Driving along this boring road uncluttered by distractions, I found myself watching the road ahead. I knew that my child's graduation and my mother's death had opened the future in ways I could not yet articulate and would only appreciate as I lived into it. The future was ahead, and I could not see it. *But* there were plans beginning to be formed. There would be a trip with my dear friend to Germany, which one year before I could not have made. There was a love relationship, turning into a commitment to living life together. Not even being fifty years old, there was a strong possibility that there would be yet two or more decades of life to live.

Driving into Atlanta, I knew the future lay ahead, but it was yet to come into its own. There would be surprises, challenges, hopes, dreams, friends, communities, some disappointments, and heartaches.

Advent is God's coming into what has been, what is, and what is yet to be. Advent is God's activity and God's way of entering human history. As death came in Advent, so did life. As sorrow came in Advent, so did freedom. As grief came in Advent, so did possibility.

God's redemption is of such magnanimity, such kindness, such generosity, such compassion that the whole earth and all that is therein reverberates with signs. God comes to redeem the present moment. God comes to hold all that is to be.

The day of judgment is the day of driving from the former days into the season that is yet to be. It is the journey of judgment in which sin, sickness, and sorrow are redeemed and which becomes the journey of grace.

We watch. We wait. We wonder.

(SUSAN HENRY-CROWE)

Prayers for Worship

CALLS TO WORSHIP

Leader: The day foretold is coming.

People: When our tired eyes will behold a fire, a blazing star in the eastern sky!

Leader: The one foretold is coming.

People: **Whose light will shine through the deepest gloom.**

Leader: The day is at hand!

People: **Your redemption is drawing near!**

(SUSAN HENRY-CROWE)[1]

Note

1. Adapted from Phyllis Cole and Everett Tilson, *Litanies and Other Prayers for the Revised Common Lectionary, Year C* (Nashville: Abingdon Press, 1994), p. 15.

(Based on Psalm 25:1-10)

One: Today, we offer you our lives, O Lord.

Many: **God, we trust you to take care of us so that those who would laugh at us or consider us foolish for believing in you will know shame, not us.**

One: Is that too much to ask when we study, seek your truth, and wait for you?

Many: **Remember the times in the past when you took care of us just as we ask you to protect us now.**

One: What do you think when we try to sweetly blackmail you into doing as we ask rather than live the lives of humility and faith to which you have called us?

Many: **It should not matter what others say or if we are accepted. You have given us love that does not end and a promise of hope.**

One: Today, we offer you our lives, O Lord, no strings attached, just as you offered your life for us all.

(WANDA BURTON-CRUTCHFIELD)

(Psalm 25:6-10 RSV)

Leader: Be mindful of thy mercy, O LORD, and of thy steadfast love, for they have been from of old.

People: **Remember not the sins of my youth, or my transgressions;**

Leader: According to thy steadfast love remember me, for thy goodness' sake, O LORD!

People: **Good and upright is the LORD; therefore he instructs sinners in the way.**

Leader: He leads the humble in what is right, and teaches the humble his way.

People: **All the paths of the LORD are steadfast love and faithfulness, for those who keep his covenant and his testimonies.**

(DAVID MOSSER)

PRAYER OF CONFESSION AND ASSURANCE OF PARDON

One: As we see the flame of hope burning on the altar before us, we should recognize how far from living this hope we are. Enter with me into a time of confession of our sins before God and one another.

All: **We are sinners, O Lord. We say we live for the hope of Christ's coming, but we do not. Instead, we have easy chairs and easy lives that keep us on safe streets in pretty places. But you want us to love vagrants and people who think that they are better than us. You would have us fight for justice and live in equity with one another. If hoping your kingdom will come means such upset, we are not sure we want a part of it. Will you forgive us for this doubt lying so quietly at our door? Will you help us to live the redemption that lies in your way? Prepare our hearts for the coming Christ Child. Prepare our hearts for the challenge of hope.**

One: Children of hope, know this day that Christ is coming. Christ is coming as a baby who alters everything and is nothing we expect. Christ is coming to redeem us and to give us hope. Accept Christ's gift of forgiveness and of hope.

(WANDA BURTON-CRUTCHFIELD)

We are watching, Redeeming God. In all times, in all places, we watch for a sign that your Redeeming One is drawing near. We keep the vigil for ourselves and for the earth, for we desire to know the time for your visitation. Only the Redeeming One can ease the load and make our burdens light. Only the Redeeming One can transform our poverty of spirit into abundance. Only the Redeeming One can restore our neglect of truth into a commitment to justice. We wait. We watch. We wonder. Amen.

(SUSAN HENRY-CROWE)

PASTORAL PRAYER

On this day of high anticipation, O God, we gather to hear the good news. Help us watch with alert eyes and with open hearts for your word that breaks in on our mundane lives. Day by day, and too often, we go through life's motions with little reflection on the great and wondrous things you provide for us at every turn. Small things weigh down our spirits and souls; we forget you and all your benefits to your people. You have made a solemn covenant with us to be your people just as surely as you will be our God. Allow us to approach your throne of grace as forgiven and redeemed people. Let us acquire the joy that is ours for the gathering. May we share the joy of Jesus with a world in deep need of the happiness that your divine hope provides. Most of all, make us again a people who listen for and receive your promise of the coming of the Lord. We pray this in the name of Jesus, our Messiah. Amen.

(DAVID MOSSER)

BENEDICTIONS

Hold us in our waiting, for you will surely come.
Keep us in our watching, for you will not be long.
Fill us in our wonder, for your redemption will bring us joy!
Amen.

(SUSAN HENRY-CROWE)

Now may the hope of Christ's coming invade our beings and shake up our world like a cosmic shift. To hope for the not-yet kingdom is to live and love and work and believe that God's redemption changes everything. Look up! The clouds will not be empty forever. Amen.

(WANDA BURTON-CRUTCHFIELD)

READINGS

Malachi 3:1-4

Luke 1:68-79

Philippians 1:3-11

Luke 3:1-6

The Messenger

MALACHI 3:1-4

Sometimes at supper my family plays the Dinner Party game. If you could invite one person—living or dead—to have dinner with us, who would it be? What would you want to talk about? And what would you serve for dinner? We dream of inviting Virginia Woolf, Queen Elizabeth, or Robert Redford. One of the favorite choices is Jesus. Among us we can think of infinite things to talk with him about. While I think we really mean to ask him infinite questions, I wonder if we'll be ready and able to hear him as well.

Somewhere in this lively exchange, I inevitably begin to look around our home. For Queen Elizabeth I'd have to lock the dogs in the basement so they wouldn't lick her legs or beg her scraps. The spare van seat parked along the dining room wall would show up symbolically in a Woolf novel. And for heaven's sake, if Jesus came, I'd really have to clean the place. This latter thought gives me such pause, rather akin to despair, that I attempt to talk the family out of these delightful invitations.

Don't get me wrong. I think housekeeping is a high calling, a respectable profession, one I practice when I'm seized with anxiety, desperation, confusion, or when friends are coming over. (I've also been known to invite people over just so we have to straighten.) There's nothing like the presence of an outsider (or even its suggestion) to help us see our own messes, to call chaos to our attention, and to get us moving. The more you unclutter, the more dirt shows and you know how much needs correcting.

Twentieth-century British mystic Evelyn Underhill wrote a lovely little reflection entitled *The House of the Soul.*[1] She notes that spiritual life mirrors rather easily the natural or domestic life; the house reflects the spirit of its inhabitant. She visits the soul's lodging, pointing out darkness, light, unexamined storage, decoration, frayed edges, dust. We have infinite ways of hiding the mess; even clever clutter attempts to cover it for others and ourselves. The messenger sees beneath the surface: "Company's coming, and we've got work to do." In any case, I am in serious trouble. We are, too.

Getting ready for Jesus demands our full attention, and we rarely give anything our full attention. Multitasking is the password for survival in our world: e-mail and phone conversations, chores and news radio, prayer and grocery lists, dinner and homework, grading papers at the dentist. It seems we must attain two rewards simultaneously to make an activity worth doing. One isn't enough anymore.

This is the role of the messenger: to capture our wandering attention, to turn our eyes homeward, and to help us perceive what needs clearing, carting away, cleaning, refurbishing. How will our spiritual houses be renewed? Even the question is a sign of hearing the message. We know our distraction, our misappropriation of love, and our selfishness. The great Purifier will do this work, at our invitation, but our focused cooperation is necessary. One thing at a time.

"O Come, O Come, Emmanuel," we sing, perhaps with little

intention to really make our homes presentable for such mean-ingful company. In that case, the Messenger reminds us: get going, take stock, make preparations! Individually and corpo-rately we have to want the purifying, to open ourselves to it, and to commit to faithful pursuit of the goal of loving God with our whole selves. We must give ourselves to this love alone, for its own sake.

Recently I taught a Sunday school class on Islam. A woman interrupted to ask, "Do you mean that they can't pray and iron at the same time?" I love that about Islam. The great confession says that God is one and means also that only that One matters. Formal prayer has its own focused and uninterrupted time, where only one duty occupies one's full attention. Christians could learn to honor God better through the purity of one thing at a time. Those asking for the presence must prepare for it, ready themselves for the gift of grace, make room for it in the midst of much life-cluttering activity and stuff.

So you want to invite Jesus to your home and heart? Is there room there for another? Is the invitation for you or will it simply honor the Messiah? What needs doing in your heart as you await the Messiah? Is the way prepared, straight and smooth, and free of damaging distractions?

A jeweler traveled to study with a Chinese jade master. On the first day of training the master blindfolded him, put a stone in his hand, said, "This is jade," and departed. At the end of the day, he wordlessly took the stone and removed the blindfold. The next day the master blindfolded him, put a stone in his hand, and said, "This is jade." The days, weeks, months went by. One day the master placed a stone in his hand, and the blindfolded stu-dent burst out, "I came to learn jade from you, the Master who knows so much. For months you simply set stones in my hand in darkness. I have had enough! And today—of all days—this stone is not even jade!" The master removed the blindfold and, smil-ing, said, "Your lessons are done. You may go now."

The Messenger calls the community to one thing—the truest of loves in relation to the Holy One and to one another. We know it fully by training, by exposure to it, in the simplicity of its practice. Unlike the student of jade, we never finish mastering this love. But we make ready again and again for the coming of the Christ, Love Incarnate in our world, in our hearts. The Messenger cries, "Prepare the way of the Lord, make the paths straight." May it be so.

(JAN FULLER CARRUTHERS)

Note

1. Evelyn Underhill, *The House of the Soul* (London: Methuen & Co. 1929).

What to Give the Baby
PHILIPPIANS 1:3-11

This is the Christmas shopping season, as everybody knows. Do I dare to be really nosy and ask you if Jesus is on your list for presents? It's *his* birthday, you know. And may I meddle further and suggest not only that you add his name, but that you place it at the top of the list? This, of course, raises major questions for serious shoppers. Just what is this preacher getting at?

Well, I'd like to offer some helpful suggestions. In the first place, most Christmas gifts are bought with money. We are jostled about in the frantic shopping crowds in order that we may lay down money for gifts, some useful and some just part of the tradition. The present says to the receiver, "This is what I felt I could afford." And many people of limited means are deeply depressed at Christmas because they don't have the money it takes to say what they want to say.

Some sensitive people in our time have taken to *making* presents with their own hands. It conveys a warmer personal message. Even if it isn't any more useful than many bought presents, a handcrafted gift shows how much of the real you, as opposed to your hard money, is in the gift. But even this requires some shopping, if just for materials and wrappings.

The apostle Paul offers an idea that would work at Christmas in a most appropriate way. You don't have to shop for it, and it is very warmly personal. In fact, it comes from within the giver—from the very depths of a person. Paul reminds the Philippians that God "has begun a good work in you" (1:6) and urges them to be "filled with the fruits of righteousness, which are by Jesus Christ, unto the glory and praise of God" (1:11 KJV). In other words, each of us has the option of pleasing our Lord on his birthday, just by seriously rededicating ourselves to continuing the work Christ has already begun in us. That work is evident in the fruits of righteousness which we live out.

People think of self-denial and spiritual discipline during Lent, but Christmas is no less a time for renewal. Indeed, the Christmas basket of the "fruits of righteousness," which Paul suggests, may very well require a wider scope of altered lifestyle. But this plan has the advantage of the positive motivation of a lovingly reordered life, offered to him as Holy Infant, who in maturity has already given us the empowerment by beginning this "good work" within us.

Paul's plan contrasts further with the all too common shopping pattern in that the latter diminishes the donor's resources. Many people mortgage a year's salary with credit purchases made for the obligatory exchange of gifts, with or without love. Others suffer through Christmas, in sorrow over their inability to lavish on their loved ones the gifts they themselves longed for as children.

Still others come to Christmas Day exhausted from the effort of observing it in the manner of our commercially influenced culture. They may have the money, but they are physically and emotionally exhausted by the effort required. I am reminded of our four children who for years gave only to Jesus at Christmas. In their early teens, they voted to conform to this "world," just to see what it was like. A "large" sum of two hundred dollars was appropriated, and small teams chose and purchased gifts for each of us. They had hardly completed one shopping expedition when they wanted out. Their frustration lay in the high prices paid for thoughtful choices that proved useless. Never again did they vote to conform to the cultural context, and they gladly received their many gifts on their own birthdays.

Paul's plan for concentrating on a basket of the fruits of righteousness for the baby Jesus has the marvelous advantage of enhancing the givers, not depleting them. Those who rededicate their lives at Christmas achieve the subtle side effect of abundant life for their "trouble" all during the ensuing year. That doesn't mean that no money is spent, but it does mean that the gifts are for Jesus, not for us and our friends. Our family delighted in breeder rabbits for Ecuador and, in later years, a gift to the Southern Christian Leadership Conference. The contents of Jesus' Christmas basket are influenced by Jesus' own advice that those who live for self lose real life and those who lose their lives for his sake will find life abundant (Luke 9:24; John 10:10*b*).

The bottom line, however, is that the gifts in the basket of righteousness not only bless the giver but have implications for the whole world. That stable boy at Bethlehem took part in the plan of salvation for the world. When, from within, Mary gave birth to that baby, her earlier song of praise was more justified than she dreamed: "From now on, all the succeeding generations will say that I was blessed to be able to give this birth" (Luke 1:48*b*, paraphrase).

Whatever other gifts accompany our fruits of righteousness and whatever they cost or don't cost, I can say after many years of trying to fill the basket that there is no greater joy and no greater fulfillment. A haunting Christmas carol from late-nineteenth-century England has a poor child summing it up by asking:

What can I give him, Poor as I am?
If I were a shepherd, I would bring a lamb;

If I were a wise man, I would do my part;
Yet what I can I give him: Give my heart.[1]

(Ella Pearson Mitchell)

Note

1. From "In the Bleak Midwinter," by Christina G. Rossetti, 1876.

And You Call This Good News?

LUKE 3:1-6

John's announcement of the Messiah's coming fell softly on no one's ears. He certainly didn't try to lull his audience into believing that they could welcome the Savior with an unreflective enthusiasm like that of a child who looks forward to Santa Claus coming to town. John the Baptist's words were troubling. Almost everything he said seemed to be calculated to provoke his hearers. He did not adorn his speech with compliments or consolations, which might have made his message more readily acceptable. The harshness of the tone made it evident that he had no patience with those who would require coaxing or cajoling before they would be receptive to his message. John spoke with brutal frankness.

The great church reformer Martin Luther once stated that the most consistent outcome of the word of God is that on its account the world is put into an uproar, for the sermon of God comes to change and revive the whole earth insofar as it really gets through to it. John no doubt put things into an uproar. Personally, I would not have wanted to bear the brunt of his preaching. He spoke of mountains being ripped down and valleys being filled up to prepare the way for the Lord. That's radical disruption.

The Christ that John the Baptist announced is certainly a

threat to anyone who has become complacent and overly comfortable with their lives, values, and opinions. The Christ that John called people to prepare for was One who came to interrupt the normal course of life in order to introduce the way of God. Jesus is that Christ, and Jesus came to disturb us. William K. McElvaney wrote a challenging little book a few years ago, entitled *Good News Is Bad News Is Good News,* in which he said,

> All my life, from time to time, I've sung "Blessed Assurance, Jesus Is Mine." These words can become little more than a sentimental exercise in reducing Jesus to our own size unless accompanied by the theme "Blessed disturbance, I am Christ's!" Not that I welcome God's disturbance when it occurs in the midst of my life. At least, though, I've learned from past experience that sometimes the news I thought was bad news turned out to be some of the best news I'd ever heard.[1]

The preaching of John the Baptist, upon first hearing, was as disconcerting as a clanging burglar alarm that shatters the sleepy silence of the night. His message sounded quite distinctly like bad news. But in fact it was wonderful news. The Christ was coming, and the people needed to be prepared to meet him, even though the preparation was going to disrupt their lives. His coming is disruptive to our lives as well. If not, then we have created a *Christ* after our own image, an idol that satisfies our desires and warms our hearts but does not move us beyond our self-centeredness.

The most crucial preparation was, and is, not ritual but ethical—not entirely internal and individualistic but external and social. Devotion to God and compassion toward those in need are indispensable if we are to prepare the way of the Lord. Hugh Kerr, past president of Princeton Theological Seminary, once observed,

> We live in a world that answers back to us. It says yes to our yes, and no to our no. The sailor must hoist his sail if he is to catch

the wind. The miner must sink his shaft if he is to discover the gold. The engineer must swing his bridge if he is to harness the river. The aviator must spread his wings if he is to search the sky. The financier must make his investment if he is to find his fortune. The Christian must prepare the way if the living God is to appear.

Let us prepare ourselves for the celebration of the coming of Jesus Christ by working for a world in which no one is ill-clad while others of us have closets filled with clothes that we throw out and replace as styles change. Let us work for a world in which no one goes to bed hungry while so many of us are thoughtlessly wasteful and self-indulgent. If we are ever to have a just and fair world, the adjustments that will be required of us privileged folks may be painful. But these are labor pains that precede a new birth of joy. There is no better way to prepare for the Lord.

(*CRAIG M. WATTS*)

Note

1. William K. McElvaney, *Good News Is Bad News Is Good News* (Maryknoll, N.Y.: Orbis Books, 1980).

Prayers for Worship

CALLS TO WORSHIP

Leader: Listen: God will send the messenger to prepare the way.

People: **Who is the One who will come after?**

All: **The messenger of God's promises, to bring us great peace and joy!**

(*ELLA PEARSON MITCHELL*)

(Based on Philippians 1:3-11)

In this place, in these approaching moments, only one thing is required of us. Rest, rest, rest in God's love. There is room here for all you are, all you bring, every concern and joy. Hear the Holy Voice say, "Come." Hear the awesome stillness. Open your heart to it, and worship the God of tender mercy who began a good work in you and will bring it to completion at the day of Jesus Christ. Come. Rest.

(JAN FULLER CARRUTHERS)

(Based on Luke 1:68-79)

Leader:	Blessed be the Lord, the God of Israel, who has come to set the chosen people free.
People:	**The Lord has raised up for us a mighty Savior from the house of David.**
Leader:	Through the holy prophets, God promised of old to save us from our enemies, from the hands of all who hate us;
People:	**to show mercy to our forebears and to remember the holy covenant.**
Leader:	This was the oath God swore to our father, Abraham:
People:	**to set us free from the hands of our enemies, free to worship without fear, holy and righteous in the Lord's sight, all the days of our life.**
Leader:	And you, child, shall be called the prophet of the

Most High, for you will go before the Lord to prepare the way,

People: **to give God's people knowledge of salvation by the forgiveness of their sins.**

Leader: In the tender compassion of our God the dawn from on high shall break upon us,

People: **to shine on those who dwell in darkness and the shadow of death and to guide our feet into the way of peace.**

(THOMAS GILDERMEISTER)

ASSURANCE OF PARDON

(Based on Luke 1:68-79)

One: Let us confess our hearts and lives before God and one another.

All: **God of compassion, we are not nearly ready to welcome you. Our preparations are late and inadequate, our hearts are distracted by worries, hopes, and material clutter. We are a disorderly people. We do not yet love justice and mercy, we do not yet seek peace, so we cannot walk as friends with you. We are sinners. Come to us, O Holy and Tender One, to forgive us and save us.**

One: Through the tender mercy of our God, the day dawns upon us from on high. God gives light to us who sat in darkness and death. God saves us, forgives us, and sends us forth from this moment on, to live as new people. Amen.

(JAN FULLER CARRUTHERS)

PASTORAL PRAYERS

All-loving and forgiving God, how long will you remain patient with us? How long will you wait for us to turn from our broken and sinful lives and take upon ourselves the mind of your Son, Christ Jesus? All you ask is for us to accept your love, accept your grace, accept your forgiveness, and fall into your arms. But we hold back. We're too busy right now, or we're this or that. God, forgive us. O Lord, have mercy. We confuse the shabby rewards of this world with the perfect and eternal rewards of Jesus Christ. We cling to our possessions as if our lives depend on them. And all the while, you lovingly whisper that our lives depend on letting this stuff go. We do not wait on your Son very faithfully at all, but we wait and we believe. Give us the faith to persist. In his holy name. Amen.

(THOMAS GILDERMEISTER)

Almighty and ever-present God, we praise and honor you this day. As John the Baptist sought to herald the bringer of salvation, inspire us to continue with love and loyalty to lift up Jesus Christ. We bless you for the invitation to a creative new adventure that can make the world a better place. We pray for strength and courage to alter the traditions that hold us so tightly. As we join in Paul's prayer that echoes down the centuries, lead us and guide us.

"And this I pray, that your love may abound yet more and more in knowledge and in all judgment; that ye may approve things that are excellent; that ye may be sincere and without offense till the day of Christ; being filled with the fruits of righteousness, which are by Jesus Christ, unto the glory and praise of God" (Phil. 1:9-11 KJV). Amen.

(ELLA PEARSON MITCHELL)

BENEDICTION

Depart from this hallowed place to bear the fruits of righteousness. And the peace that passeth all understanding be yours, through Jesus Christ, to whom be glory, honor, and praise forever and evermore! Amen.

(*ELLA PEARSON MITCHELL*)

READINGS

Zephaniah 3:14-20

Isaiah 12:2-6

Philippians 4:4-7

Luke 3:7-18

God Sings

ZEPHANIAH 3:14-20

Are you ready for a merry Christmas? For many folk, a "merry" Christmas seems far out of reach. We don't always acknowledge it, but many people are weighed down by unhappiness at this time of year. Some are grieving the death of a loved one, some are battling depression or addiction, some are entangled in painful family dynamics, and some are weary with illness. Some are worried about looming problems on the global scene. Some haven't paid much attention to God in a long time and resent the reminders of God's presence around every decorated corner. Some feel like God couldn't care less. Indeed, a lot of folk aren't too joyful. And to be honest, can we blame them? Can we even acknowledge the true difficulties in our own lives with "Joy to the World" sung every time we turn on the radio?

The prophet Zephaniah wrote to a people weighed down in the aftermath of the oppression of the Assyrian Empire. Their political and religious leaders had bowed to foreign leaders and foreign gods. The poor and the outcast were ignored while people pursued worldly wealth. Corruption and violence ran rampant from the courthouse to the sanctuary. The people grew so weary of the moral stench and spiritual vacuum in which they lived that they had become indifferent to God. They didn't think God could make a difference in their lives—not in their grief, their poverty, their fear, or their shame.

God called Zephaniah to speak a word from the Lord to these ancestors of our faith who had lost their trust in God. Yet the first two and a half chapters of the book of Zephaniah hardly sound like words of comfort to a people in captivity. Zephaniah speaks harshly on behalf of the Lord, especially admonishing the leaders for their waywardness and their lack of trust in God. God is fiercely angry, Zephaniah warns. God will consume the earth in the fires of his passion (1:18). The great day of the Lord is coming. Instead of "Joy to the World," Zephaniah sings "Wrath to the World," the Lord is coming!

But wait. Something changes. God relents. Zephaniah ceases words of warning and destruction and gives birth to new hope with words of comfort. Maybe God remembers that we humans cannot restore ourselves on our own; perhaps God's parental heart breaks at the thought of continuing to punish these precious children. Regardless, Zephaniah stops telling the people what they've done wrong and starts telling them what God is doing right. "Rejoice!" Zephaniah says. "Look what God is going to do for you! Your judgment has been taken away. God is with you! You don't have to be afraid anymore. God is victorious over all of your enemies. And God will sing a song of rejoicing over you!"

Then—another change—the text shifts from Zephaniah speaking for God to God speaking for God's own self! Zephaniah has told us there would be a song, and God begins singing it! "I will save you," God sings to the people, "I will help the lame and the outcast, and I will lift up those who are ashamed. I will bring you home and give you everything you need!" The voice of God lifts off the printed page and becomes a resounding love song for all to hear. It turns out that God yearns for joy, too, and is willing to step in and do for us what we cannot do for ourselves so that we can live in joy.

A few years ago I was visiting a member of my congregation at the Veterans Administration hospital. I was waiting with him in a patient holding area, where many others were waiting for various tests and procedures. Our visit was interrupted by the sound of a man groaning loudly and the softer sound of a woman humming. As the noise continued, I excused myself from our visit and followed the sound of the groaning and the singing. I turned the corner to see a badly scarred man lying on a gurney, groaning and speaking nonsensically. Beside him sat a woman, stroking his brow and humming gently to him. I introduced myself and asked if I could sit with them for a few moments. The woman seemed glad for the company. She told me their story. He had been wounded in Vietnam, resulting in severe mental and physical handicaps. "He's been like this ever since," she ended. My mind raced to do the math—for thirty years they had suffered like this. I was speechless. Finally, I asked, perhaps selfishly, "If you don't mind me asking, how have you endured?" She smiled and said, "I know that one day God's gonna come and heal him. And I intend to be here when he does." And she began humming again.

I'm not sure, but I think that in the sound of her humming song, I heard the sound of God singing, too. She was humming the tune that fits the promise we find here in Zephaniah. It was just the beginning, but it was a hint of the loud love song to come. It was the first bars of a ballad of boisterous victory over sin and disease and oppression and all that keeps us from joy. It was the lullaby of a mother comforting her child; it was the raucous tune of a warrior when he has won the battle. I'm not sure, but I think that in the sound of her humming song, I heard the sound of God singing, too.

Perhaps then "Joy to the World" is not the song for those of us who cannot find much joy this time of year. Perhaps "It Came

Upon a Midnight Clear" is a more genuine expression of our faith. This Advent, you who are "beneath life's crushing load," "rest beside the weary road, and hear"—not just the angels singing—but our great God Almighty, singing over you.

(DAWN DARWIN WEAKS)

Rejoice Always!

PHILIPPIANS 4:4-7

My sister shared with me a quaint saying from her German neighbor: "Be sure to listen to people who sing while they work, 'cause mean people don't know no songs." The saying seemed extreme at first, but the more I thought about it, the more sense it made.

Paul's admonition likewise seems extreme at first. Could he be serious about this business of rejoicing all the time? To find out, let's look at the context in which he says it. Two very faithful women of the Philippian church are not of the same mind. This is a gross understatement: their disagreement is tearing up the church. When it was just beginning, these sisters were dependable and hard workers. "But now that the church done growed bigger, they done fell out over somethin', an' they ain't even speakin' to one another." Paul is deeply concerned; Jesus just might be back any time, and here this leading church is all torn with dissension.

"Beloved, please do what you can to help these sisters settle this argument so the church can get back to the work of the gospel. The rest of the saints are getting restless, and we can't cover up this struggle. The whole community knows about it. So we just have to find some kind of settlement to bring back peace and harmony. They both see themselves working for the Lord, but not together. And that makes it look like they are working for themselves."

Paul's most emphatic advice to his yokefellow (whoever this is), and to the church at large, is to rejoice. If you look at all you have to praise God for, you won't know how to hold your mouth to fuss at anybody. You can count your blessings or count your criticisms. But blessings give God the praise that is due, while negative statements make a sour face and drive people away.

Many years ago there was a member in our congregation who hated my husband with such a passion that she ordered him never to set foot on her property. We never found out why. But she did have one fine trait: she was an all-out worker for civil rights. One day my husband was running a big demonstration in 106-degree weather. This sister drove up beside him and gruffly ordered, "Get in this car before you kill your fool self." He obeyed and sat quietly watching her from the corner of his eye. What he saw was a woman too happy with the success of the demonstration to be mad at anybody. She tried to frown and failed. She had to break down and laugh as she drove him to the front of the line and wished him well. Rejoicing had taken the wind from her jaws and the meanness from her heart.

We fuss to let off the steam of our frustration and anger, and we use it to hurt and subdue people. We may say it is because we have to express righteous indignation, but our fussing is a weapon in a personal war. It is a way of putting people down, but it keeps us down.

In Dickens's *A Christmas Carol,* old Scrooge discovers that the put-downs heaped on his bookkeeper only help destroy his own peace. When he is finally scared by ghosts into joining Tiny Tim in rejoicing, shouting "Merry Christmas," he is made happier than he has ever been. Perhaps the greatest, really Christian aspect of Christmas in our culture is the fact that for many, it is the most joyous season of the year.

If we really want to bring peace and harmony, and help the family and the church, fussing will not do it, but rejoicing will. People do more good things because they are glad than because they are mad. Paul is urging the creation of a joyous Christian fellowship in which it is easy to do right, because one is already happy.

Then Paul follows the admonition to rejoice with a word about witness. "Be known to everyone for your consideration of others" (v. 5 REB). It is a powerful witness for the Lord, who will soon return. We can't afford to waste time and influence. Jesus' joy is contagious, and we are on "candid camera" all the time. If we do not witness for our joy in the Lord, we are witnessing for the reverse.

I suppose the most contagious joy and powerful witness I ever saw was at a university commencement. The governor had spoken, and the solemn assembly had moved to the reading of the names of the graduates. Suddenly a name was called, and a lady screamed, "Glory! Glory!" Her large white hat went sailing, and she shouted with an ecstasy such as few people ever enjoy. She herself would never have had such joy if she had felt compelled to hold it in. She did what Paul said and let it out. Joy isn't joy until you express it.

Paul's advice wasn't so strange after all. May you learn to rejoice in the Lord this Advent as you have never rejoiced before. And may your main joy come from the good news of God with us, starting at the manger.

(*ELLA PEARSON MITCHELL*)

Concrete Compassion
LUKE 3:7-18

John the Baptist is trouble during Advent. Most come to worship wanting to sing familiar Christmas carols, hear about the Christ Child, and feel good inside. John offers none of these comforts. Rather, John is the madman of the desert. Rather than comfort, he offers attack. Instead of praise for participation in the religious customs of the time, he suggests stones could be made more faithful. While it might be affirming to praise the worshiper for attendance, John instead questions their motives and calls them poisonous snakes. The preacher is tempted to turn to the Old Testament or epistle lesson for some more palatable material for the growing Christmas crowds. Is it possible that the choir might sing a cantata this week instead of having a sermon?

Yet, the lectionary and the gospel offer no escape from John's harsh words. Facing them might not be pleasant or popular, but the faithful must face them. Many preachers are reluctance to deal with these texts. While John may have gotten away with attacking his listeners, the preacher is not John the Baptist. The best starting point with dealing with texts of this sort then is to acknowledge our own discomfort with the text and the way it attacks, and then seek God's work in a hard word. For when one listens beyond the harsh rhetoric of John's preaching, one can hear a message most of us need to hear. In this sermon, John is addressing a subject with which all faithful people struggle. How does one appropriate the lofty ideals and stirring phrases of the faith with the practical everyday realities of life in the world? This is John's theme, and it is a message needed during the holiday season.

John's admonition is simple. We are to put our idealism to work in everyday acts of compassion, justice, and simple living. Certainly at holiday gift-giving season, there is a word from God calling God's people to simple lifestyles. Too much holiday gift giving is a poorly disguised trading of luxuries among the affluent. John would have us give to the poor and live more simply ourselves. Justice is the theme of John's word for the tax collectors. How might we do justice this season? A look at any newspaper or report offers many illustrations of the need for justice workers during Advent.

John's message is one each generation needs to hear. Instead of getting caught up in the trinkets and trivia of the holidays, God longs for those who can keep to the business of the faithful. God calls for repentance from the self-serving ways we practice as holiday festivities. God calls us to concrete acts of compassion that have more substance than a dollar or two in the collection plate for the needy at Christmas. Christian discipleship is much more than romantic visions of babes in the manger in the Advent season. Compassion, justice, and simplicity are harder now than in any other month of the year. They are also more holy.

(CARL SCHENCK)

Prayers for Worship

CALLS TO WORSHIP

Leader: Sing, be glad and rejoice with all your heart!

All: **The Lord, the Creator of all life, is with us.**

Leader: Be not afraid, O daughters of Zion.

All: **The Lord our God will give us peace and goodwill, for the Prince of Peace is come.**

(ELLA PEARSON MITCHELL)

(Based on Isaiah 12:2-6)

Leader: Come, give thanks to the Lord; call on God's name. Let every nation know the mighty deeds of our God!

People: **Surely God is our salvation.**

Leader: People of God, the Holy One is in your midst.

People: **Let us sing praises to the Lord. Let us shout aloud and sing for joy!**

(DAWN DARWIN WEAKS)

(Based on Isaiah 12:2-6)

Leader: Surely God is my salvation;

People: **I will trust, and will not be afraid, for the Lord God is my strength and my might; he has become my salvation.**

Leader: With joy you will draw water from the wells of salvation.

People: **And you will say in that day: Give thanks to the Lord, call on his name; make known his deeds among the nations; proclaim that his name is exalted.**

Leader: Sing praises to the Lord, for he has done gloriously; let this be known in all the earth.

All: **Shout aloud and sing for joy, O royal Zion, for great in your midst is the Holy One of Israel.**

(DAVID MOSSER)

PRAYER OF CONFESSION

O God, like the children of Israel, we have strayed from the path of righteousness, and our hearts have enshrined the idol of material gain. We have treated Jesus' birthday as if it were our own, and we have taught our children to seek for self, rather than to yearn to bring gifts to their Lord. We have rejoiced in small things given to us and overlooked the true joy of our Savior, laid in a manger for our sakes. Forgive us, we pray, and teach us the true joy of Christmas, and indeed, the joy of praising you throughout the year. Amen.

(ELLA PEARSON MITCHELL)

ASSURANCE OF PARDON

We will give thanks to you, O Lord, for we thought you were angry with us, and now we know your anger has turned away (Isa. 12:1). We will sing praises, for this day is come the Son of Righteousness, the messenger of your forgiveness. Amen.

(*ELLA PEARSON MITCHELL*)

PASTORAL PRAYERS

O God, you are our deliverer and our salvation. We give thanks this day that you are not deterred from coming to our aid by our indifference or our lack of trust in you. Though we have ignored you and turned our trust to lesser gods, you have never given up on us. We acknowledge in these quiet moments that you are the one true God, and we yearn to be your faithful people once again. Restore to us the joy of our salvation. Help us, O God, to turn to you more quickly when we are afraid and to rely on you more fully when we have decisions to make. Give courage to those who fight against temptation. Give relief to those who bear the burden of grief. Give hope to those who struggle with illness. Give reassurance to those who doubt you. Prepare us by your Holy Spirit to receive the gift of Jesus Christ, our Savior, once more. Amen.

(*DAWN DARWIN WEAKS*)

This is a day of rejoicing. O Lord, teach us to pray with your great apostle Paul who wrote, "Rejoice in the Lord always; again I will say, Rejoice" (Philippians 4:4). Out of this great joy of salvation, given to us as a free gift in Christ Jesus, let us remember the poor and the needy. Everything we have and hope to be comes from your gracious hand, O God. And because you have made us stewards, help us fulfill this role in your realm. We want to be better people, but sometimes life makes our path difficult. Give us the courage to look at people like Mary and Joseph and be inspired by what they willingly sacrificed for their dream of a just and peace-filled world. Fill us with your spirit during this season as we prepare our hearts, minds, and lives for the coming of the Messiah. Let us prepare the Christ a place in our lives so that he may reign in us and for us. We pray this in Jesus' holy name. Amen.

(DAVID MOSSER)

BENEDICTIONS

(Based on Philippians 4:4-7)

Rejoice in the Lord. Let God carry the burdens of your heart. And the peace of God, which surpasses all understanding, will guard your hearts and minds in Christ Jesus. Rejoice in the Lord!

(DAWN DARWIN WEAKS)

Joy to all, the Lord is come. Peace to all, the Prince of Peace is with us. Live now as children of grace, and may the love of Christ shine through you, this day and always. Amen.

(ELLA PEARSON MITCHELL)

READINGS

Micah 5:2-5*a*

Luke 1:47-55

Hebrews 10:5-10

Luke 1:39-45 (46-55)

Who Would Have Ever Thought?

MICAH 5:2-5*a*

Micah was a prophet of the Southern Kingdom of Judah. He had a sense of God's impending judgment as a consequence of the hateful injustice of the people. It is a time of controversy and uneasiness especially in light of the work of Isaiah in the north and the fate of the Northern Kingdom. Micah's message announces God's certain judgment to be sure, but there is also an element in his message of signs of hope for the future. Our Advent passage is taken from that promise of a futuristic hope.

The message for our consideration is one of God's actions in the midst of doom and despair. Micah seeks to remind the people that although judgment is imminent, God will bring forth from that judgment a hope that will not only bring God's peace to Judah but also to the world. Micah makes it clear that this promise of a new ruler will find its beginning in the smallest of places, Bethlehem. The emphasis here is on what God can do with the smallest, the least likely. Such a brilliant prophecy seeks to use that which is unlikely to become the tool of God's blessing of hope. This device places the focus on the power of God and what God can do with very little. Certainly as we wait and watch we need to remember that God will be at work in the places and through the people we least expect. Such seems to be the way of God. This theme needs to be part of the message we seek to proclaim in this season of Advent.

In Viktor E. Frankl's book, *Man's Search for Meaning*, he tells a story that illustrates how God shows up in the strangest and most unexpected ways. Frankl was a prisoner in a Nazi concentration camp during World War II. He tells of how he and some other prisoners were moved on a work detail from Auschwitz to a Bavarian work camp.

> One evening when we were already resting on the floor of our hut, dead tired, soup bowls in hand, a fellow prisoner rushed in and asked us to run out to the assembly grounds and see the wonderful sunset. Standing outside we saw sinister clouds glowing in the west and the whole sky alive with clouds of ever-changing shapes and colors, from steel blue to blood red. The desolate gray mud huts provided a sharp contrast, while the puddles on the muddy ground reflected the glowing sky. Then, after minutes of moving silence, one prisoner said to another, "How beautiful the world *could* be!"[1]

This is the message of Micah in the face of despair and impending doom. Micah reminds the people of God that somehow, someway, God will once again redeem and reclaim that which is broken, lost, hurt, wounded, destroyed. Even in the midst of death and dying, through a sunset, God reminded a group of prisoners not to give up hope, for indeed the world could be beautiful!

This Advent people need to hear once again that hope is possible through the constant, loving, redeeming work of God. Our watching and waiting this season needs to be focused where we many times forget to look. It is such a paradox that during

Christmas, when we should be celebrating all that is right with the world, it becomes so easy to lose ourselves and lose sight of what is important among self-imposed deadlines, meaningless traditions, and ridiculous expectations. Micah reminds the people to look to Bethlehem for their future hope. Who would have ever thought to look to Bethlehem?

(*TRAVIS FRANKLIN*)

Note

1. Viktor Frankl, *Man's Search for Meaning* (New York: Washington Square Press, 1964), 62-63.

The Mystery Ahead
HEBREWS 10:5-10

As we come to the final Sunday in Advent, the anticipation of welcoming anew the Christ Child reaches its zenith. As we prepare to give in to the great joy of the celebration, this scripture passage surprises us. It reminds us that the mystery of the incarnation makes sense only in light of the paschal mystery. We celebrate the birth of Jesus only because of the death and resurrection of Jesus. Advent and Christmas point ahead to the cross. This text is a pointer.

I. Remaining in Christ

The anonymous writer of Hebrews seeks to sustain persons, predominantly Jewish Christians, who are wavering and in danger of abandoning their faith. The writer seeks to persuade them to remain in Christ by assuring them that God has acted decisively and finally in history to make them acceptable before God. Redemption and sanctification by the work of Christ are spoken of in the perfect tense. The work is complete. There is no need for remediation or repetition. By means of interpretation of all three portions of the Jewish Scriptures, Jesus is shown to be superior to the angels, to Moses, to the Levitical priesthood, and, in this biblical passage, to the sacrificial system.

II. Why Read This at Advent?

On first consideration, this lection seems out of place in this season of the liturgical year. Familiar Advent themes such as preparation, expectation, and hope are absent. Yet it may correct the way in which we focus upon Christ's coming, especially if we are prone to being too sentimental over the baby Jesus. Hebrews is identified by many commentators as a sermon from the early Apostolic Age (as early as 52–54 C.E.) celebrating the significance of Christ. As such, it reminds us that the early church found Jesus' significance not in his birth, miraculous though it may be, but in his obedience unto death. This drove their interpretation of him. What is more needed at Advent?

III. Be Careful!

A great temptation to which Christians have fallen repeatedly, with disastrous consequences, is the idea that Christianity has superseded the Jewish faith. Hebrews, with its language of Christ's superiority to key aspects of the Jewish religion, is especially liable to be interpreted in this way. Indeed, Hebrews has been used to underwrite much supersessionist theology. We need to take care to avoid this.

Sensitivity to such issues may lead some to question Hebrews. Does it somehow disqualify itself? The use of the Jewish Scriptures to interpret Jesus, such as in Psalm 40, affirms his continuity with the Jewish faith. Indeed, it places Jesus the Jew, who is the same "yesterday and today and forever" (Heb. 13:8), within the Jewish context for all time. However, understanding Hebrews involves working within yet another Advent tension.

This time the tension is that of the real and proper joy over the birth of Jesus and the realization of what lies ahead.

The dual themes of welcoming the baby Jesus in knowledge of what awaits him was expressed in stunning fashion by W. H. Auden in his Christmas oratorio, "For the Time Being" (which is excellent spiritual reading for Advent). Auden lets us hear Mary's anxieties in the words she speaks to her newborn son: "In your first few hours of life here, O have you Chosen already what death must be your own? How soon will you start on the Sorrowful Way? Dream while you may."[1]

Such is an appropriate Advent word for we who in baptism receive new life by being united with him in death.

(PHILIP E. THOMPSON)

Note

1. W. H. Auden, *Collected Longer Poems* (New York: Random House, 1969), 171.

Mary's Song
LUKE 1:39-45 (46-55)

Mary, why are you singing? Child, you should be weeping. You're pregnant, betrothed to an honorable young man who knows this is not of his doing. Why aren't you sobbing on your knees, crying inconsolably?

Such a child yourself. Perhaps you sing because you are so young, but even children know when they have broken the law. You've seen how people treat those who break social mores: raised eyebrows, turned heads, chuckles whispered behind cupped hands. You will be shunned at best, stoned at worst. Have you noticed how the nice girls aren't quite so friendly anymore?

Poor one, have you any idea where all of this will lead you?

Away from home for your confinement, next door to an inn of rowdy strangers, in a crude shelter for your first birthing. Poor one, little do you know about that not so merry chase your boy child will lead you on as he goes about his father's business. Beginning at the temple in Jerusalem, it will end at Golgotha. Perhaps it is best you do not know the future. Sing on, little innocent.

But child, have you any idea what the words mean? How radical your lyrics? What makes you think a woman-child would be noticed by the mighty Yahweh, let alone magnified! Be careful who hears you. This could be blasphemy!

Naive and childish boasting is one thing, little maid, but singing revolutionary lyrics in Roman territory is quite another. Your song moves from flirting with sacrilege into a whole new arena of politically incorrect and inflammatory statements. You have entered a land where few maidens dare to tread, the land of politics and economics. You sing of God's strength scattering the proud. (Mary, the proud don't like to be scattered, haven't you heard?) You sing that God has put the mighty down from their thrones. (This might be good news to the powerless, but not to the mighty. How long do you think rulers will let you sing songs like this?) The hungry have been filled with good things, and the rich have been sent away empty. (The rich don't like to be empty, Mary. They won't sing along!)

Perhaps you should stop singing, child. Should this song capture the imagination of the poor ones, they will turn the world upside down. Mary, for your sake and the child's, keep a lower profile. Think a minute, is this the kind of mother you want to be—a troublemaker, setting this example? Will you rock your baby to sleep with lullabies like this and make him radical too? What if he remembers and teaches others, and it catches on, and on and on, so that two thousand years later the melody lingers and we must ask ourselves:

People of God's family, why are we singing today? What is there within the human heart that brings forth song when the news of this present world contradicts good tidings and cannot begin to define the meaning of great joy? And yet the song goes on. Why will it not be silenced?

Perhaps it is the power of expectation, having something to dream in the darkness. Birth is like that. And this is a song of birth, of a miracle incapable of rational description, a song staccatoed by the kick of tiny feet, a song filled with hope for a child yet unseen.

Young girl, how desperately we need your song! We need your song in hospital rooms and state rooms, in our kitchens and in outer space, reminding us of God's timeless refrain:

God is vital, active—in today and tomorrow.

God is fresh as birth—with potential as promising as a babe.

God loves justice, blesses the merciful, feeds the hungry.

God comes to us—unreasonable, unpredictable, unbelievable.

God comes to us in the middle of tax season, to the poor ones, making promises yet to be fulfilled.

God comes to us in Jesus, and Jesus gives God a face.

This is the song. God is with us, then and now and yet to be. And because God is with us, there is something to look forward to, something unseen, something called hope!

There are children diseased and dying who paint rainbows and sing without reason. Or is the reason hope?

Old folks clean house and plant gardens between bombings in the war zones of our world. They have no reason to sing. Or could it be hope?

Hungry ones repair to their larders and find only two loaves of bread remain, yet they sell one and buy white hyacinths to feed their souls. They sing with half filled stomachs. Is this hope?

The world looks at dying and war and hunger, and cries, "There is no hope! There is no song!" But Mary sings, pointing to rainbows and gardens and hyacinths. And the song of Mary echoes beyond disease and bombs and empty stomachs.

So, little Mary, sing! You're expecting. And we too shall sing of the unborn dreams kicking within us waiting to be born. "It isn't yet . . . it is yet to be."

For Mary sings of Jesus before his birth. But there is no question in her mind, he will be born. Mary sings of God's justice before righteousness reigns throughout the world, but there is no question it will come to be. In spite of the fact that the rich are still rich, the poor are still poor, and the hungry are still starving, justice is sung as a melody complete, already fulfilled.

God has already shown strength, scattered the proud, put down the mighty, exalted the lowly, filled the hungry. This has happened and yet—it hasn't happened yet. This is and yet—it is yet to be. Can it be the promises of prophecy grow as real and as hidden as the fetus gestating toward the fullness of time: Not yet, but yet to be? Not yet realized, but real? Not yet delivered, but pregnant?

We, the Advent people, are waiting, seeing the real world, but singing anyway. Singing with the blind, whose eyes are yet to be opened, because we know God believes in vision.

We, the Advent people, are waiting, hearing the real world, but singing anyway on behalf of the deaf, whose ears are yet to be unstopped, because we know God will be heard.

We, the Advent people, are waiting, dancing a stumbling sort of gait along winter sidewalks and honking our way down busy streets because we know someday the lame will leap into the circle with our Lord and the whole world will join the dance.

And somehow, in this sad and muted world, we are called to speak, no, we are called to sing on behalf of those who are dumbfounded. We are to sing because we believe God wills us to harmonize with the angels those old familiar tidings of great joy.

So sing, Mary. Go ahead, sing. Lead us in your song. Amen.

(SYLVIA C. GUINN-AMMONS)

Prayers for Worship

CALLS TO WORSHIP

(Adapted from Micah 5:2-5a)

Leader: Our God comes to us as a baby in a manger.

People: **Our God comes as a shepherd to feed the flock.**

Leader: The shepherd will stand in the strength of our God,

People: **And the name of the shepherd is Love.**

Leader: The child shall be great to the ends of the earth,
People: **And the name of the child is Peace.**

(JUDITH FAGALDE BENNETT)

Leader: O sing to the Lord a new song, for God does marvelous things!

People: **God hears us and remembers us with steadfast love and faithfulness.**

Leader: Make a joyful noise to the Lord, all the earth!

People: **Glory to God in the highest heaven, and on earth good news for all.**

(SYLVIA C. GUINN-AMMONS)

(Based on Luke 1:47-55 RSV)

Leader: My spirit rejoices in God my Savior,

People: **For he has regarded the low estate of his handmaiden.**

Leader: For behold, henceforth all generations will call me blessed;

People: **For he who is mighty has done great things for me, and holy is his name.**

Leader: And his mercy is on those who fear him from generation to generation.

People: **He has shown strength with his arm,**

Leader: He has scattered the proud in the imagination of their hearts,

People: **He has put down the mighty from their thrones, and exalted those of low degree;**

Leader: He has filled the hungry with good things, and the rich he has sent empty away.

People: **He has helped his servant Israel, in remembrance of his mercy,**

Leader: As he spoke to our fathers,

All: **To Abraham and to his posterity for ever.**
(DAVID MOSSER)

(Canticle of Mary)

Leader: My soul proclaims the greatness of the Lord,

People: **my spirit rejoices in God my Savior, who has looked with favor on me, a lowly servant.**

Leader: From this day all generations shall call me blessed:

People: **the Almighty has done great things for me and holy is the name of the Lord, whose mercy is on those who fear God from generation to generation.**

Leader: The arm of the Lord is strong, and has scattered the proud in their conceit.

People: God has cast down the mighty from their thrones and lifted up the lowly.

Leader: God has filled the hungry with good things and sent the rich empty away.

People: God has come to the aid of Israel, the chosen servant, remembering the promise of mercy, the promise made to our forebears, to Abraham and his children for ever.

(THOMAS GILDERMEISTER)

PRAYER OF CONFESSION (IN UNISON)

Holy child, born of a singing mother,
Forgive us our monotone lives,
for seeing darkness rather than light,
for hearing bad news rather than magnificent music,
for living with dread rather than delight.
Redeem us, enliven us.
Give us hope in our hearts and a song on our lips. Amen.

(SYLVIA C. GUINN-AMMONS)

ASSURANCE OF PARDON

We need only ask and our prayer is heard. We need only hope and a promise is kept. God hears us and keeps us. Friends, believe the good news of the gospel. In Jesus Christ, we are forgiven.

(SYLVIA C. GUINN-AMMONS)

PASTORAL PRAYERS

Come Thou long-expected Jesus, we sing as a prayer, dear Lord. Now let it be so. We have awaited this day the whole long year. The joy of this season and its anticipation are deep within our bones. O Lord, you know we sing better, we feel better, and we pray better as we wait for your coming with expectation. We become almost like children as we anticipate the fulfillment of your ancient promises in the Christ whom you have named Jesus. Like Joshua of old, may he be for us the one who leads us toward and into the land of promise. Remind us to care for the lonely and alienated this Advent and Christmas season, O Lord. For it is in our sharing that we find our truest selves. We want to be your people, so incline our ears to the story of the good news found in our Scripture. May we, in these holy days, live lives that befit the gospel. May we spread the good news by the cheer we share with those who have little. Remind us that it is more blessed to give than to receive. We pray this in the holy name of Jesus, our Messiah. Amen.

(DAVID MOSSER)

The eve of Emmanuel! O dear God, precious Savior, we fidget and fret with impatience. We want peace in our world dropped in our laps. We want justice for all to fall out of the sky. And we aren't willing to do your legwork. We act as though either you haven't called us to love our neighbors or we don't *really* believe that you are coming again. We punch our tickets with an embarrassed response to an altar call, and then sit on our hands. God, forgive our need for lazy, simplistic answers to the world's woes. Give us the heart of Christmas, not only during this season of pomp and celebration, but every day of the dreary winter, the hopeful spring, the doldrums of summer, and the musty autumn. Give us a new heart, sweet Jesus. Amen.

(THOMAS GILDERMEISTER)

BENEDICTIONS

(Adapted from Luke 1:46-55)

Go now to await the birth of the Holy Child, whose mercy is for those who fear him from generation to generation. Find ways in this season to lift up the lowly and fill the hungry with good things. And let *your* soul magnify the Lord and your spirit rejoice in God our Savior. Go in peace. Amen.

(JUDITH FAGALDE BENNETT)

Christians, go into the world with a song in your heart. And may the God we know as Creator, Christ, and Comforter sing through you always. Amen.

(SYLVIA C. GUINN-AMMONS)

READINGS

Isaiah 9:2-7

Psalm 96

Titus 2:11-14

Luke 2:1-14 (15-20)

The Christmas Eve Zoo

Luke 2:1-14 (15-20)

One church had two Christmas Eve services. One service started at 11 P.M. with only a faithful few. It was quiet, with deep, dark, ponderous silence, reflective liturgy that matched the plethora of candles, and Holy Communion from silver. You could almost hear angels singing across the windswept "Silent Night." The church's other Christmas Eve service began at 7 P.M. with lots of rowdy children scrambling everywhere in a flurry of velvet dresses and bow ties being chased by weary parents in casual pants and bright Christmas sweaters. Though we sang "Silent Night" during the candle lighting ceremony at the end, it was hardly silent. It was a zoo.

Though there's a part of us that craves the deep reflective silence of the 11:00 service, the 7:00 service is probably more faithful to Luke's story of Jesus' nativity where we have a cast of characters that makes Jesus' birth look like a zoo.

Consider the familiar story again. What a strange group of characters Luke presents to us. Look at all the different species of humankind roaming through Luke's Gospel like different animals in a modern-day zoo wandering through a common savannah. Luke's Gospel opens with the ubiquitous secular powers roaring in the background. "In the days of King Herod," "a decree went out from Emperor Augustus," "while Quirinius was governor." It's as though Luke is warning us never to forget that, in the background of this story, lions of power lie in wait. But there's another often overlooked character in the cast of nameless crowds of people praying and hoping for deliverance: a crowd that roams as prolific through Luke's Gospel as antelope mulling about on the savannah. Then there's Zechariah, a priest doing temple duty as one of the religious elite, steady as an elephant, a well-respected member of his community whom everyone knew, kind of like a pastor of a small town. Then we have Zechariah's wife, Elizabeth, the blue-blood daughter of a priest, who with God's help gets pregnant at last with John the Baptist, a character who leaps into Luke's Gospel like the wild man of the jungle, looking as wild and woolly as a gorilla. Then along strolls Mary like a beautiful giraffe, a young girl who says to God's wild proposition, "Let it be with me according to your word," despite the fact that under the law she should be put to death for being with child by someone other than her betrothed Joseph. And Joseph! Good ol' "just Joe" cheated out of his lovely bride but who nonetheless saves and protects her, a man who doesn't see things as black and white as a zebra but one who understands the nature of God's law as based upon mercy. Then there are the scruffy shepherds who show up after the birth of the child, veritable jackals, hardened folk with a reputation for criminal activity. Shepherds were marginal people— poor, down-on-their-luck, children put to work early. Yet can't you see them—grizzle-faced, gently holding the baby, wide brown-toothed grins that match the smiles of everyone else who takes up a baby in this story.

So many different human characters all gathered around the most common human element—a baby, the baby Jesus. And that's just the cast of *human* characters in Luke's nativity story—not to mention the all-powerful God who steals the show or the angels hovering over everything like a morning mist rising from an earth being transformed by good news of God's new work, singing "Glory to God in the highest!" My goodness, so many different folk! Were they not frozen like little statues in our romantic nativity scenes, these different species of folk wouldn't get along for more than fifteen minutes. So many different characters; it's a zoo.

Maybe that's the point, God's ludicrous point—a baby born right in the middle of this zoo called humanity. For in the center of all is a bawling baby filled with God's Spirit who came to clean up the elephant-house stench of sin that we live in so that all God's creatures could live in harmony as intended without the need for bars between us. When you think about it, being born in a manger among the animals is an apt description of God acting in our human situation structured by the sin of a dog-eat-dog world to transform it into one in which a lamb can sleep peacefully with a wolf instead of ending up as dinner. So now instead of devouring one another, with the coming of the Christ Child, we can serve one another the feast of God's new creation born with Christ our paschal lamb, splayed out in all the vulnerability of a newborn baby whose innocent death on the political cross of lions forces us to look upon the mess we've made of this thing called life, to take responsibility for our sin forgiven by the power of God, and to be transformed through the working of God's Spirit Way. Maybe that's the point of this zoo-like configuration of characters: God at work among the animals. God gathering the whole of a rowdy, raucous humanity around an innocent babe in a feeding trough.

(*Teresa Lockhart Stricklen*)

Prayers for Worship

CALLS TO WORSHIP

(Based on Isaiah 9:2-7)

Leader: The people who walked in darkness have seen a great light; those who lived in a land of deep darkness—on them light has shined.

People: You have multiplied the nation, you have increased its joy; they rejoice before you as with joy at the harvest, as people exult when dividing plunder.

Leader: For a child has been born for us, a son has been given to us;

People: And he is named Wonderful Counselor, Mighty God, Everlasting Father, Prince of Peace.

[Move to the lighting of the Christ candle on the Advent wreath.]

(TERESA LOCKHART STRICKLEN)

Leader: Sing unto the Lord a new song.

People: Sing God's praises in the assembly of the faithful. For the Lord enjoys our worship.

Leader: Sing unto the Lord a new song.

People: For Jesus is born this night in Bethlehem, and all of heaven and all of earth are rejoicing.

(VIVIAN ROBERTS)

PRAYER OF ADORATION AND CONFESSION

Holy Child, born of Mary in a barn, you identify with us in abject humanity. You move among us with announcements of good news when things look bleak; you give us a star on dark, lonely nights. Sing to us once more that, assured of your presence among us, we may forget our fear and embrace your gift of newborn life, to the glory of your holy name we pray. Amen.

(TERESA LOCKHART STRICKLEN)

INVITATION TO HOLY COMMUNION

So come, let all us different folk adore him. Good religious folks, scruffy shepherds, blue-bloods, young women, good ol' Joes, children, seekers after truth, come. Bring your bulletins and your candles, and let's gather around the newborn babe. Help one another as needed (for those who have difficulty walking). Those of you who cannot stand can sit on the outside edge of the pew—whatever works. But let the circle be unbroken. Come, let us adore Emmanuel.

("O Come All Ye Faithful" can be sung as people gather in a large circle that encompasses the sanctuary's perimeter.)

(TERESA LOCKHART STRICKLEN)

PRAYER OF CONFESSION

Leader: Almighty God, you caused our beginning. You have always been involved in our lives; you are always ready to receive us into your presence. You came among us in Jesus, our brother. Hear now our confession to you:

People: **We confess that we are often more ready to respond to you in your house of prayer than we are to respond to you in our daily lives. Preoccupied with the successes and failures of our daily lives, we not only miss the opportunity to see you, but we also miss the opportunity to share your love with others. Forgive us, enable us to be more open to you, and guide us always. Amen.**

(VIVIAN ROBERTS)

ASSURANCE OF PARDON

Through the life, death, and resurrection of Christ, God cleanses us and gives us power to proclaim the mighty deeds of the One who called us out of darkness into light. As a called and ordained minister of the church of Christ, and by his authority, I declare to you the entire forgiveness of all your sins, in the name of the Father, and of the Son, and of the Holy Spirit. Amen.

(BARBARA BERRY-BAILEY)

BENEDICTIONS

(Based on Isaiah 9:2 and 60:1)

The people who walked in darkness have seen a great light; those who lived in a land of deep darkness—on them light has shined. *[The pastor lights her candle from the Christ candle, then passes it around the circle with all singing an appropriate hymn.]* Arise, shine, for your light has come, and the glory of the Lord has risen upon you. *[Close by singing "Joy to the World."]*

(TERESA LOCKHART STRICKLEN)

May the brilliant floodlight of the one who called us out of darkness shine on you, in you and through you, that you may go from this place and lighten someone else's darkness. Amen.

(BARBARA BERRY-BAILEY)

READINGS

Isaiah 52:7-10

Psalm 98

Hebrews 1:1-4 (5-12)

John 1:1-14

Word Became Flesh

JOHN 1:1-14

My youngest son was born on Christmas Day at 2:48 P.M.—a time that brought unspeakable joy to my mathematician husband. The clock said 2:48 (two to the first power—2, two to the second power—4, and two to the third power—8). Needless to say, this put my husband in mathematical heaven.

This baby, like my first son, would change my life and the life of my husband. Neither of us took it lightly that he was born on Christmas Day, and just as we did with our other children, we had great visions of how he would change the world and how he would make a difference for justice in the universe. Though I would probably have fallen short of Mary's Magnificat, I could very well have stood in the street both times that I was pregnant and shouted great revolutionary predictions for change in the world order. Most mothers feel this way.

I say "most," because motherhood is not always a welcome

event for women—especially not for poor, unwed mothers, engaged to be married, who find themselves pregnant by someone other than their intended spouse. In a place where choice is possible, such a woman might choose not to bear a child.

I often wonder what the world would say if today Jesus were to come to such a woman. Perhaps a woman like some of the women I have met in the homeless shelters or the dinner programs or in the soup kitchens. What would happen if God chose them to bear a child? How differently would the world react? Would there be wise men coming from faraway just to see this child, no doubt living in one of the ghettos of the inner city, or in the barrios, or on the reservations, or in the Appalachian mountains, or in a trailer park? Is this generation ready for a Christ who would come under these circumstances?

It is on this Christmas Day that we should reflect on the story in which the "Word became flesh." It is the embodiment of the Word in the form of Jesus that we celebrate. And what has that Word been through the ages? The Word has been consistent. Whether it found its place in the Ma'at of the Egyptians, the Code of Hammurabi, or the Hebrew Bible, God has made known through many manifestations, that it is the oppressed, those that are held captive, the widow, the orphan, that deserve preferential treatment.

God's option for the poor and the oppressed comes through once again as this Christmas story emerges. This is not a story about gifts of material wealth. Indeed, it is just the opposite. It is about a gift of spiritual wealth, a gift so rich in spirit that it draws wise men and sages from near and far to witness the presence of the world's greatest paradox. A king born in a manger, a pregnant virgin, a son of God born of humans, a fully divine and a fully human baby. This paradox continues to confound the wise. So they come looking but not knowing why God chose a manger and a poor Palestinian girl to bear the labor pains that would give birth to a child who would change the world.

If in this day and time God chose once again to bring forth Christ in the womb of the welfare mother, the prostitute, the crack addict, the homeless woman, the mentally disabled, the physically disabled, the poor, the destitute, ask yourself, this Christmas Day where would you go to find him? Do you know where these women are in your community? Do you know how to find them? If you knew, would you go and seek them out? If you knew that Jesus was their newborn baby, would you be afraid to go to the housing projects to see him, to the prison, to the barrios, to the ghettos, to the reservation? How much more different today is that trip than the one taken to the manger by the three wise men long ago?

Christmas is a time for joy, but at what expense are we joyous? As you open the gifts, as you repeat the story, remember that God chose Mary to bear Jesus.

(*LaVerne M. Gill*)

Prayers for Worship

Calls to Worship

(Psalm 98, adapted)

Leader: Make a joyful noise to the Lord all the earth; break forth into joyous song and sing praises.

People: **Sing praises to the Lord with the lyre, with the lyre and the sound of melody.**

Leader: With trumpets and the sound of the horn make a joyful noise before the King, the Lord.

People: **Let the sea roar, and all that fills it; the world and those who live in it.**

Leader: Let the floods clap their hands; let the hills sing together for joy.

All: **Let all the world sing praises to a just and powerful God.**

(LaVerne M. Gill)

Prayer of Confession (in unison)

Gracious and just God, you cared enough to rescue us from our faithlessness. You cared enough to give us hope in the midst of our hopelessness. Yet we have failed to live as people whose spirits are renewed. We have failed to dispense justice wisely. We have lost our way, and we seek to be found and to be healed and to be made whole. We pray for personal wholeness and for worldly justice. In the name of Jesus Christ we pray. Amen.

(LaVerne M. Gill)

Assurance of Pardon

Leader: God has never left us. God has never forsaken us. God is with us. Believe the good news. You are forgiven.

People: **Alleluia, Alleluia, Alleluia. Amen.**

(LaVerne M. Gill)

Benediction

Go now, knowing that the Lord is with you. Know that the Lord is for you. Know that the Lord is here. Go now singing Immanuel. Immanuel. God is with us. Immanuel. Amen.

(LaVerne M. Gill)

READINGS

1 Samuel 2:18-20, 26

Psalm 148

Colossians 3:12-17

Luke 2:41-52

Following Samuel's Example

1 SAMUEL 2:18-20, 26

In an interview, renowned West Coast furniture maker Sam Maloof told how a young man came to him seeking an apprenticeship. Unfortunately, there was no room for another up-and-coming woodworker to study with this master, so Sam called his friend George, who works in Pennsylvania. The young man and George spoke over the phone. Sadly, the interview went poorly. The young man reported that George wouldn't take him.

"Why not?" asked Sam.

"He said, 'I could not teach you to sweep my floor in three months.' I told him I already knew how to sweep floors. And then he just hung up on me."

Sam said the young man should have said, "If it takes a year, I want to learn how to do it."

In the Old Testament, Samuel was in Yahweh's service. There was never any question of "How long?" unlike the cries of the psalmist. Samuel did what was required of him. He didn't live at home with his brothers, sisters, mother, and father. And yet, he was at home. His mother continued the family ties, making him coats and taking them to him on the annual excursion to the temple at Shiloh. It's like sending homemade cookies to a child in college or at seminary.

Whenever anyone asks me how I came to enter the ministry, I invariably tell a little story: When I was five years old, I was playing on the front porch at my maternal grandmother's house. She and Mom were talking about this and that. At some point, Grandma placed her pudgy little hand on top of my head and said to my mother, "Eric is going to be a minister when he grows up."

"Over my dead body!" retorted Mom, who knew from past experience what a difficult task lies ahead for ministers and their families. Even I couldn't see myself preparing a sermon a week, much less getting up in the pulpit on Sunday morning and preaching. I was going to be a musician, or a psychologist, or an English teacher, not a preacher.

The first day of seminary classes, the professor asked us to introduce ourselves and to say why we came to seminary. Everyone had something nice to say. Finally, it was my turn. I told the class where I'd gone to school and made the usual introductions. The professor asked me why I had come to seminary. "To spite my mother," I replied. Needless to say, she wouldn't have me doing anything else.

Here is Samuel, growing in stature and favor. As Samuel increases, not only does Eli begin to decrease in importance, but so do Eli's sons, Phinehas and Hophni. They lose face before God as Samuel surpasses them, standing in stark contrast to his mentor's children. He practices what they in their greed and lust for power had long since forgotten, that silence isn't really silent and even darkness has bold luminosity for those who wait on it. The window of opportunity is flung open for God to sweep in and call out to young Samuel, who is something of an essentialist. That is, he is gripped by the realization that there is a given nature from which many of us have become estranged—God. Hophni and Phinehas have become separated from God, and God's fury is expressed in willful destruction of these two failed servants.

(Eric Killinger)

Be-Attitudes for a New Millennium

COLOSSIANS 3:12-17

The end of the twentieth century brought with it "the cultural equivalent of an earthquake," as one scholar put it. Now we face the rebuilding of the predominant Western civilization into a new global civilization, with new sensitivities and emphases. How will we, the church of the living God, speak to these realities? The scripture for today speaks to this question.

I. Be Positive

In the preceding verses, Paul describes what must be "taken off" and rejected by the Christian. Most non-Christians and many Christians regard faith as primarily negative in content, like the boy Stephen in Clyde Edgerton's *Where Trouble Sleeps:* "A lot of it—getting saved—had to do with visiting old people and going to church every time you were supposed to . . . and not drinking beer and whiskey. And it had to do with not saying ugly words, not running away from your mama . . . and not playing in the mud."[1]

In verses 12-13, Paul turns to a positive note, providing the runway commentary for a Christian fashion show. The "laundry list" of virtues that a Christian wears is lovely, and any decent commentary will help you to explicate the textures of these virtues. The primary emphasis here is that God chose us to go into his own closet to choose our wardrobe!

II. Be Perfect

The difference between a nice wardrobe and a stylish look is the "tied-together" style of the accessories. In the case of the Christian, love is the attitude that brings the parts of our characters into a single whole. Love, in the words of one writer, is "not an emotion but a policy." Just as wood putty fills cracks and defects in wood so that the wood might be useful, so love covers the individual defects and idiosyncrasies in our faith so that we can be useful to God. As described in *The Message* translation, love is our "basic, all-purpose garment" (v. 14).

III. Be Peaceful and Thankful

Living at peace with other Christians is sometimes difficult. Noah had as much to fear from the woodpecker inside the ark as he did the storm outside. Our "umpire of conduct," paraphrasing the Greek, is the rule of peace. "Will my action promote peace in the church?" is an excellent guide to contributing to the progress of each church. The corollary to this question is that of thankfulness: Will I, will God, be thankful for how I conducted myself toward fellow believers? The refusal to behave in a peaceful manner toward others, coming out of gratitude toward God, results in a loss of harmony in our own hearts.

IV. Be Praise-Full

The "culture wars" of the 1990s invaded the church, so much so that division rather than diversity characterized the dispute over the proper style of worship. In this scripture, Paul proposes a basis for unity in this endless debate: If it is in harmony with the Word, it is appropriate for worship. If the word of Christ dwells in you, then whether you sing psalms or gospel songs, praise choruses or anthems, have a praise team or a robed choir, is of little importance. If the word of Christ is not in you or your praise, your praise is hollow anyway. Worship is the only remedy to the irrelevance of the twenty-first-century church, for only God is the only constant priority in the history of the church.

IV. Be Purposeful

The name of Jesus Christ is the center of our Christian living. His name provides both our identity ("I am a Christian") and our authority ("I do this in Jesus' name") for our conduct. As a Christian acting in his name, I need not cower nor bully, neither whine nor despair. I am adequately prepared for what lies ahead.

(*MICKEY KIRKINDOLL*)

Note

1. Clyde Edgerton, *Where Trouble Sleeps* (Chapel Hill, N.C.: Algonquin Books, 1997),

Not Home Alone

LUKE 2:41-52

I can't help thinking of the movie *Home Alone* when I read Luke 2:41-52. Of course the star of the story is not Kevin, the little boy left behind when his family left on vacation, but Jesus. In the bustle and confusion of getting ready for a trip, he gets left behind in Jerusalem. Jesus' mother, Mary, was even slower than Kevin's mother to realize the child was missing. Instead of a few hours, it took a whole day for Jesus' parents to notice that his passenger seat was empty.

The family had been in Jerusalem for the Passover, the most important religious holiday of the year for Israel. After the festivities, they packed to head back home to Nazareth, their hometown. Jesus' family was traveling with a group of others. Apparently his parents thought he was with some other people. I can imagine the shock they must have felt when they realized they had left him alone in the big city.

It took Mary and Joseph three days to find Jesus. Three days of anxiety, tears, and guilt, I imagine. I can hear it all now: "We should have been paying more attention. We should have been absolutely certain he was with us. How could we have left him there? What rotten parents we are."

But after three days of frantic searching, they neared the great Temple. They turned a corner and there he was. He wasn't crying and worried. He didn't blame his parents for neglecting him. No, instead Jesus was sitting with the teachers, the religious experts, asking questions and listening to their answers. It seems that the people who had heard Jesus had been pretty impressed with what he had to say.

His parents were more appalled than impressed. When they saw that Jesus was not frightened or in any kind of danger, they got upset in a different way. Parents are like that, kids. Sometimes if they think you're lost or in trouble and then they find out that you're all right, they don't know what to do first, hug you or spank you for not listening to them in the first place. It seems that's the way it was with Mary and Joseph. When they found Jesus, his mother said, "Child, why have you treated us like this? Look, your father and I have been searching for you in great anxiety." In other words, "Jesus, we've worried ourselves to death because we thought you were lost. You should be ashamed of yourself for making us feel so terrible." Have your parents ever talked to you like that, kids?

Well, what did Jesus say? "Mom, Dad, I'm sorry. I'll never do something like that again." Is that what he said? No, what he said was, "Why were you searching for me? Did you not know that I must be [about] my Father's [business]?" Jesus' earthly father, Joseph, was a carpenter. Jesus wasn't sitting there with a saw and hammer. He was talking about not his earthly father's business but that of his heavenly father, God. Jesus had left his parents and caused them a lot of worry by going to the Temple to get involved in divine business.

What do you think about that? Those of you who are parents, I know what you think. You'd go wild if your child tried a stunt like that. So would I. Most of you who are still living with your parents probably wouldn't want to be left in a big city without your folks. But if you did ever take off on your own without permission for a little unsupervised adventure, chances are you know you'd face a lot of love but also plenty of trouble when you got back home. Let's be clear about this: The lesson we can learn from this episode in Jesus' life is not that it's all right to take off on your own without your parents' permission. There are some lessons that this story about Jesus does suggest.

First, there is something more important than parents and families. Jesus realized this early in his life, and he taught it later as an adult. He said, "Whoever loves father or mother more than me is not worthy of me; and whoever loves son or daughter more than me is not worthy of me" (Matt. 10:37). God is first.

One time when Jesus was preaching in front of a crowd, Mary got concerned. She came with some of Jesus' brothers to get him. Some of the people told Jesus his family was looking for him. What did Jesus say? He said that his mother and brothers are those who hear the word of God and do it (see Matt. 12:46-50). Jesus loved his family, but he knew that doing what God wanted him to do was the most important thing ever. Kids and parents need to know this as well.

Second, kids, you need to be patient with your parents. Someone once said that a child becomes an adult three years before his parents think he does and about two years after he thinks he does. Some parents really don't know how to let their children grow up. Not long ago I heard a fifty-year-old woman say, "My mom is still trying to tell me how to live my life." It happens.

Third, listen to your parents. Even though Jesus did fine in Jerusalem all on his own, when his parents told him how upset they were, he paid attention. The Scriptures tell us that when he went back home with his folks, he "was obedient to them" (v. 51). It's tempting to close your ears to your parents when they say things you don't want to hear.

Maybe you feel that you know more than your parents. Sometimes you might be right. Jesus certainly knew more than his parents. Can you imagine raising the son of God? Still, he listened to his earthly parents.

(CRAIG M. WATTS)

Prayers for Worship

CALLS TO WORSHIP

(Psalm 148 RSV)

Leader: Praise the LORD! Praise the LORD from the heavens, praise him in the heights!

People: **Praise him, all his angels, praise him, all his host!**

Leader: Praise him, sun and moon, praise him, all you shining stars!

People: **Praise him, you highest heavens, and you waters above the heavens!**

Leader: Let them praise the name of the LORD! For he commanded and they were created.

People: **And he established them for ever and ever; he fixed their bounds which cannot be passed.**

Leader: Praise the LORD from the earth, you sea monsters
           and all deeps, fire and hail, snow and frost, stormy
           wind fulfilling his command!

**People: Mountains and all hills, fruit trees and all
           cedars!**

Leader: Beasts and all cattle, creeping things and flying
           birds!

**People: Kings of the earth and all peoples, princes
           and all rulers of the earth!**

Leader: Young men and maidens together, old men and
           children!

**People: Let them praise the name of the LORD, for
           his name alone is exalted; his glory is above
           earth and heaven.**

Leader: He has raised up a horn for his people, praise for
           all his saints,

**All: For the people of Israel who are near to
           him. Praise the LORD!**

                                          (*DAVID MOSSER*)

(Based on Psalm 148:1-14)

Leader: Praise the Lord! Praise the Lord from the heav-
           ens, praise the Lord, in the heights!

**People: Praise the Lord, all his angels, praise the
           Lord, all his hosts!**

Leader: Praise the Lord, sun and moon, praise the Lord,
           all shining stars!

People: **Praise the Lord, highest heavens, and all waters above the heavens!**

Leader: Let them praise the name of the Lord, who commanded and they were created,

People: **who established them for ever and ever, and fixed their bounds which cannot be passed.**

Leader: Praise the Lord from the earth, sea monsters and all deeps,

People: **fire and hail, snow and smoke, stormy wind fulfilling God's command!**

Leader: Mountains and all hills, fruit trees and all cedars!

People: **Beasts and all cattle, creeping things and flying birds!**

Leader: Kings of the earth and all peoples, princes and all rulers of the earth!

People: **Young men and maidens together, old men and children!**

Leader: Let them praise the name of the Lord, whose name alone is exalted, whose glory is above earth and heaven.

People: **God has raised up a horn for his people, praise for all his faithful ones, for the people of Israel who are near their God. Praise the Lord!**

(*THOMAS GILDERMEISTER*)

PASTORAL PRAYERS

O God of the Holy Family, you have baptized us into the faith of Christ and given us the task of being your people. Give us this day the power of Christ's spirit as we worship you, Creator, Sustainer, and Redeemer. In you we find our true center and in you, O Lord, we find our meaning and value for life. May we all participate in the life of our church and be baptized evangelists of the good news. May our words and actions invite others to be a part of the Christian life. Grant us a fresh spirit and give us a portion of your divine energy to live fully in the life that Christ offers us. As we worship this day, may our hearts and minds turn toward divine things. Create in us an enthused spirit to share good tidings that we ourselves have heard and received. Let the mind of Christ be ours. We pray this in Jesus' holy name. Amen.

(DAVID MOSSER)

How surprising is your wisdom, Holy Christ! We praise you for turning the tables and keeping us a little off balance, but we plant ourselves too firmly in our ways of living. We rarely can hear the faithful and wise words of the children. Too often we find reasons to stay away from this community of faith. Some here today are reluctant to become a part of any church. Too many "good reasons" not to commit. O Lord, open our eyes and ears so that the joy of church is evident; so that the blessing of study is clear; so that the songs and Scriptures of old brim with newness and meaning. Dear God, many resolutions will be made in the next twenty-four hours. By your grace, may we all resolve to follow Christ into your house and out into the world to love you, know you, and serve you in all that we do. In the name of the Messiah, the Christ Jesus. Amen.

(THOMAS GILDERMEISTER)

READINGS

Isaiah 60:1-6

Psalm 72:1-7, 10-14

Ephesians 3:1-12

Matthew 2:1-12

The Messiah

MATTHEW 2:1-12

In Solomon's quest for wisdom (1 Kgs. 3:1-15), the Hebrew Bible says that he asked for a discerning *labab*. Translated, *labab* means mind or heart. This blurring between the words mind and heart has its genesis in the non-western Hebrew cultural context in which mind and heart are joined together as a repository of wisdom and compassion. Thus, Solomon's request is not only for wisdom in the traditional Hebrew sense; Solomon has asked for something else. He is responsible for the lives of many people, so many he can hardly number them. In this grand scheme of things, Solomon needs a new kind of wisdom.

What Solomon seeks, Jesus, according to Matthew's Gospel, already has. We find in the visit of the three wise men to the baby Jesus respect for their wisdom tradition but also the recognition that they are moving from a point of prominence in the world of the wise to a point where they are only observers of the new wisdom. Jesus, the new creation in human compassion and wisdom, has been made manifest. He has appeared.

This epiphany is more than just the appearance of *a* Messiah, though. This is *the* Messiah, the one who comes as the Son of God to take away the sins of the world. He *is* wisdom and compassion. No longer will the meaning of wisdom be the same, and so the wise men pay homage to the future. They pay homage to the new way of knowing, the new way of revelation, the new way of performing signs, this time through miracles.

The wise men sojourn and make their way to the new keeper of wisdom, Jesus, by way of the stars. Avoiding all evil that may taint the journey and its purpose, the wise men refuse to take part in Herod's plot to kill Jesus. Satisfied with their encounter with the newborn babe, they journey home in another direction.

This new way of knowing finds its voice in the Epistles, as well. Paul, in Ephesians 3:1-12, tries to make it clear that his knowledge of Jesus Christ is not the same as that of the apostles. His knowledge does not come from books, from experience, or from being an eyewitness. His knowledge comes from revelation. It is the message from Christ through the Holy Spirit that creates in him a determination to be a prisoner for Christ Jesus, and that places him in ministry to spread the gospel to Jew and Gentile alike. It is a new kind of knowing. It is a new kind of being. Never again will knowledge, wisdom, and compassion be the same. Compassion will cease to be sentimental and placid, wisdom will cease to be contained in learning and studying, both will cease to be the province of a select few. It will be the possibility and availability of wisdom with compassion that will speak to the hearts and minds of many without a place in the society.

The wonder of the presence of Jesus, the epiphany, the manifestation of Christ in the world as God's Son, is that hearts and minds will be touched by divine revelation through the Holy Spirit. The revelation of God's manifestation in the form of Jesus Christ forces us to recognize how grand this two thousand-year-old mystery is, even in this day and age.

With all our information technology, there is nothing that

compares to the knowledge, the revelation, and the presence of the Christlike mind and heart in the world today. It has endured for nearly two thousand years and has yet to be replicated, contradicted, or proved to be less than true.

God made manifest to the world, the true wisdom. The true vine. Someone greater than Solomon has come. Praise God. Praise God. Praise God.

(LaVerne M. Gill)

Prayers for Worship

Calls to Worship

(Based on Isaiah 60)

Leader: In a world where silence and darkness linger,

People: Arise, shine, for the light has come.

Leader: In a world where sadness and fear remain,

People: The glory of the Lord has risen upon us.

Leader: Let the nations and peoples, our sons and daughters, gather together,

People: Rejoice and give thanks for the abundance around us.

All: Let us be radiant; let our hearts thrill and rejoice. Let us proclaim the incarnate Christ, the light of all. Let us worship God.

(Amy Louise Na)

(Adapted from Psalm 47)

Leader: Clap your hands and shout to God with loud songs of joy.

People: **For the Lord, the Most High, is awesome, a great king over all the earth.**

Leader: Shout to the Lord. And sound the trumpet.

All: **Sing praises to God, sing praises, sing praises to our God, sing praises.**

(LaVerne M. Gill)

PRAYER OF CONFESSION/ ASSURANCE OF PARDON

(Based on Ephesians 3:1-12)

Leader: With full and contrite hearts, let us bow our heads and confess our sins together. Let us pray.

All: **Gracious God, who gave us your son, our Savior, you shine upon us and bless and increase our lives. Yet we fail to follow your ways. We neglect your message and its saving grace for ourselves, and we doubt it for our neighbors. Teach us your mysteries and help us to forgive, as you forgive us. We pray through Jesus Christ our Lord. Amen.**

Leader: Sisters and brothers, children of God, hear and believe that the mystery of God's grace and the promise of God's forgiveness are for you. In accordance with God's eternal plan in Jesus Christ, we are forgiven. Amen. Thanks be to God.

(Amy Louise Na)

ASSURANCE OF PARDON

Leader: Know that you are forgiven in Christ Jesus. That your sins have been removed by the birth and the death and resurrection of the only true Son of God, Jesus Christ, born of Mary. In this Christ, you are forgiven.

People: **This is indeed good news. Amen.**

(LaVerne M. Gill)

PRAYER OF CONFESSION (IN UNISON)

We confess now that we have not sung your praises loud enough, O God. We have not said "thank you" enough for the many blessings you have bestowed upon us. We have not witnessed enough to a world in need of knowing your goodness. We confess that our sin has been a sin of omission. We have left you out of our witness and out of our story. We ask for your forgiveness, God of mercy and of grace. Amen.

(LaVerne M. Gill)

BENEDICTIONS

Jesus said, "I am the light of the world. Whoever follows me will not walk in darkness, but will have the light of life." May the light of the Messiah guide you through the dark and the mystery of this day and every day. Amen.

(Amy Louise Na)

We leave knowing that God, through grace, gave us Jesus for the atonement of our sins. We leave knowing that the light that was brought into the world with the birth of Jesus still shines for a world in darkness. We leave knowing that in Christ Jesus we have gained victory over death and been assured abundance in life. We leave committed to telling the story. Amen.

(*LaVerne M. Gill*)

Revised Common Lectionary Texts for Advent and Christmas Seasons, Years A, B, and C

YEAR A

First Sunday of Advent
Readings: Isaiah 2:1-5; Psalm 122; Romans 13:11-14; Matthew 24:36-44

Second Sunday of Advent
Readings: Isaiah 11:1-10; Psalm 72:1-7, 18-19; Romans 15:4-13; Matthew 3:1-12

Third Sunday of Advent
Readings: Isaiah 35:1-10; Psalm 146:5-10 or Luke 1:47-55; James 5:7-10; Matthew 11:2-11

Fourth Sunday of Advent
Readings: Isaiah 7:10-16; Psalm 80:1-7, 17-19; Romans 1:1-7; Matthew 1:18-25

Christmas Eve
Readings: Isaiah 9:2-7; Psalm 96; Titus 2:11-14; Luke 2:1-14 (15-20)

Christmas Day
Readings: Isaiah 52:7-10; Psalm 98; Hebrews 1:1-4 (5-12); John 1:1-14

First Sunday After Christmas
Readings: Isaiah 63:7-9; Psalm 148; Hebrews 2:10-18; Matthew 2:13-23

Epiphany of the Lord
Readings: Isaiah 60:1-6; Psalm 72:1-7, 10-14; Ephesians 3:1-12; Matthew 2:1-12

YEAR B

First Sunday of Advent
Readings: Isaiah 64:1-9; Psalm 80:1-7, 17-19; 1 Corinthians 1:3-9; Mark 13:24-37

Second Sunday of Advent
Readings: Isaiah 40:1-11; Psalm 85:1-2, 8-13; 2 Peter 3:8-15a; Mark 1:1-8

Third Sunday of Advent
Readings: Isaiah 61:1-4, 8-11; Psalm 126; 1 Thessalonians 5:16-24; John 1:6-8, 19-28

Fourth Sunday of Advent
Readings: 2 Samuel 7:1-11, 16; Luke 1:47-55 or Psalm 89:1-4, 19-26; Romans 16:25-27; Luke 1:26-38

Christmas Eve
Readings: Isaiah 9:2-7; Psalm 96; Titus 2:11-14; Luke 2:1-14 (15-20)

Christmas Day
Readings: Isaiah 52:7-10; Psalm 98; Hebrews 1:1-4 (5-12); John 1:1-14

First Sunday After Christmas
Readings: Isaiah 61:10–62:3; Psalm 148; Galatians 4:4-7; Luke 2:22-40

Epiphany of the Lord
Readings: Isaiah 60:1-6; Psalm 72:1-7, 10-14; Ephesians 3:1-12; Matthew 2:1-12

YEAR C

First Sunday of Advent
Readings: Jeremiah 33:14-16; Psalm
25:1-10; 1 Thessolonians 3:9-13;
Luke 21:25-36

Second Sunday of Advent
Readings: Malachi 3:1-4; Luke 1:68-
79; Philippians 1:3-11; Luke 3:1-6

Third Sunday of Advent
Readings: Zephaniah 3:14-20; Isaiah
12:2-6; Philippians 4:4-7; Luke 3:7-18

Fourth Sunday of Advent
Readings: Micah 5:2-5*a;*
Luke 1:47-55; Hebrews 10:5-10;
Luke 1:39-45 (46-55)

Christmas Eve
Readings: Isaiah 9:2-7; Psalm 96;
Titus 2:11-14; Luke 2:1-14 (15-20)

Christmas Day
Readings: Isaiah 52: 7-10;
Psalm 98; Hebrews 1:1-4, (5-12);
John 1:1-14

First Sunday After Christmas
Readings: Samuel 2:18-20, 26;
Psalm 148; Colossians 3:12-17;
Luke 2:41-52

Epiphany of the Lord
Readings: Isaiah 60:1-6;
Psalm 72:1-7, 10-14; Ephesians 3:1-
12; Matthew 2:1-12

Calendar Dates for First Sundays of Advent, 2005–2014

2005 - November 27
2006 - December 3
2007 - December 2
2008 - November 30
2009 - November 29
2010 - November 28
2011 - November 27
2012 - December 2
2013 - December 1
2014 - November 30

Old Testament

1 Samuel 2:18-20, 26 . . . 225	Isaiah 61:10–62:3 139
2 Samuel 7:1-11, 16 115	Isaiah 63:7-9 55
	Isaiah 64:1-9 75
Isaiah 2:1-5 3	
Isaiah 7:10-16 33	Jeremiah 33:14-16 163
Isaiah 9:2-7 129	
Isaiah 11:1-10 13	Micah 5:2-5a 201
Isaiah 35:1-10 23	
Isaiah 40:1-11 89	Zephaniah 3:14-20 189
Isaiah 60:1-6. . . . . . . 67, 149	
Isaiah 61:1-4, 8-11 101	Malachi 3:1-4 175

New Testament

Matthew 1:18-25 37	Luke 2:41-52 229
Matthew 2:1-12 . . . . . 68, 69,	Luke 3:1-6 181
153, 237	Luke 3:7-18 194
Matthew 2:13-23 58	Luke 21:25-36 167
Matthew 3:1-12 16	
Matthew 11:2-11 27	John 1:1-14 . . . . 49, 221
Matthew 24:36-44 7	John 1:6-8, 19-28 107
Mark 1:1-8 93	Romans 1:1-7 35
Mark 13:24-37 81	Romans 13:11-14 5
	Romans 15:4-13 15
Luke 1:26-38 120	Romans 16:25-27 118
Luke 1:39-45 [46-55] . . . 205	
Luke 2:1-14 [15-20] 43,	1 Corinthians 1:3-9 78
131, 215	
Luke 2:22-40 143	Galatians 4:4-7 141

Ephesians 3:1-12 151

Philippians 1:3-11 178
Philippians 4:4-7 192

Colossians 3:12-17 227

1 Thessalonians 3:9-13 . . 165
1 Thessalonians 5:16-24 . . 105

Hebrews 2:10-18 56
Hebrews 10:5-10 203

2 Peter 3:8-15a 91

James 5:7-10 25